THE SAINTS SHALL JUDGE THE WORLD, AND OTHER SERMONS

By Daniel Cawdrey

COPYRIGHT INFORMATION

The Saints Shall Judge the World, and Other Sermons
By Daniel Cawdrey

Introduced by C. Matthew McMahon
Edited by Therese B. McMahon
Transcribed by Blake Gentry

Copyright © 2014 by Puritan Publications and A Puritan's Mind

Some language and grammar has been updated from the original manuscript. Any change in wording or punctuation has not changed the intent or meaning of the original author(s), and has been made to aid the modern reader.

Published by Puritan Publications
A Ministry of A Puritan's Mind
2633 Lantana Road
Crossville, TN 38572
www.puritanshop.com
www.apuritansmind.com
www.puritanpublications.com

All rights reserved. No part of this publication may be reproduced, stored in a retrieval system or transmitted in any form by any means, electronic, mechanical, photocopy, recording or otherwise, without the prior permission of the publisher, except as provided by USA copyright law.

This Print Edition, 2014
Electronic Edition, 2014
Manufactured in the United States of America

ISBN: 978-1-62663-093-2
eISBN: 978-1-62663-092-5

/ The Saint's Shall Judge the World, and Other Sermons

TABLE OF CONTENTS

THE SAINTS SHALL JUDGE THE WORLD, AND OTHER SERMONS 1

    COPYRIGHT INFORMATION 2

    TABLE OF CONTENTS 3

    MEET DANIEL CAWDREY 4

    ORIGINAL TITLE PAGE 8

    THE SAINTS SHALL JUDGE THE WORLD, or A REMEDY AGAINST LAWING 9

    A CLOSE HYPOCRITE DISCOVERED 60

    THE LAWFULNESS OF DOING GOOD OUT OF HOPE OF REWARD 102

MEET DANIEL CAWDREY
By C. Matthew McMahon, Ph.D., Th.D.

Daniel Cawdrey (1588–1664)[1] was the son of Mr. Robert Cawdrey, a Reformed minister of the Gospel, who struggled greatly with the Bishops in the Church of England for his nonconformity. Daniel was the youngest of his sons. He was educated in Peter-House, in the University of Cambridge. Information regarding his life is lacking greatly, but we do know he was mightily converted to Christ for the truths of the Reformed Faith and eminently distinguished in his day in the character of a Christian minister. He was minister at Little Ilford, in Essex, in 1624. Afterwards, he settled at Great Billing, in the county of Northampton, in England.

Dr. Edmund Calamy says, "He was a considerable man, eminently learned, and a noted member of the Assembly of Divines." He became one of the leading members of the assembly of divines appointed by parliament in 1643 for the regulation of religion. He was one of the Presbyterian ministers who signed the address to the Lord General Fairfax

---

[1] Cawdrey is also spelled in some documents as *Cawdry*.

remonstrating against all personal violence against the king. At the Restoration he was recommended to Lord Clarendon for a bishopric. He sometimes preached to the members of Parliament. In a sermon preached to the House of Commons, from Prov. 29:8, at their solemn fast, he testifies against these seminaries of sin, stage-plays (what we would consider theaters today), which are often well attended, when many churches are almost empty. Speaking of open scorners, who are professed mockers of religion, he says, "Among these you may reckon your *Stage-players,* who had scoffed Religion out of countenance with many. *You have done well to put them down, and shall do better, if you keep them down.*"

This eminently good man, and faithful servant of Jesus Christ was cast out from Great Billing by the Act of Uniformity, after he had been a very laborious minister of the gospel there for about thirty-six or thirty-seven years. He moved afterward into Wellingborough, where one of his daughters was married. There he lived in great pain, receiving, however, all who came to him, and encouraging them in the ways of holiness and piety, until October 1664, when he fell asleep in the Lord; aged forty days short of seventy-six years.

Cawdrey was an able and voluminous writer of controversial divinity, both against the Anglicans on the one side, and the independents on the other; and he wrote against two of the ablest advocates of both, Henry Hammond and John Owen. Almost all of Mr. Cawdrey's written works have been published by Puritan Publications. His works are:

1. *Humility the Saints' Livery.* Substance of two sermons, from 1 Peter 5:5. London, 1624.

2. An Assize sermon at Northampton, in 1627, from Psal. 69:9.

3. *Superstitio Superstes.* 4to. 1641.

4. *The Good Man a Public Good.* A sermon preached from Prov. 29:8, to the House of Commons. 4to. pp. 43. London, 1643.

5. *Vindiciae Clavium.* or, A Vindication of the Keys of the Kingdom of Heaven, into the hands of the right Owners. 4to. pp. 90. London, 1645. in English.

6. *The Inconsistency of Independency with Scripture etc.* A threefold Discourse. 4to. pp. 219. Lon. 1651.

7. *Sabbatum Redivivum.* or, *The Christian Sabbath Vindicated.* A large and elaborate work, in two quarto volumes. The

first Part by him and Mr. Herbert Palmer; the second Part by Mr. Cawdrey alone. London, 1645.

8. *Independency a great Schism.*

9. A Diatribe against Dr. Hammond, on Superstition and Festivals.

10. A Vindication of this Diatribe.

11. *A Sober Answer to a Serious Question.* Against Mr. Giles Firmin.

12. A sermon at Paul's, July 1st 1655 from 1 Tim. 1:19. London, 1655.

13. *Self-examination for Preparation to the Lord's-table.*

14. *Family Reformation Promoted.* Small book, London, 1656.

15. *Church-Reformation Promoted.* Small book, London, 1657.

16. Bowing to or toward the Table Superstitious.

17. *An Essay against Usury.*

18. *The Grand Case, with Reference to the New Conformity.*

Meet Daniel Cawdrey

ORIGINAL TITLE PAGE

THREE SERMONS:

1. A Commission for a Court, granted to the saints.
2. A Close Hypocrite Discovered.
3. The Lawfulness of Doing Good Out of Hope of Reward.

By Daniel Cawdrey,
Rector of Great Billing in Northampton-shire.

"Let nothing be done through strife or vain glory, but in lowliness of mind let each esteem other better then themselves," (Philippians 2:3).

London,
Printed by *R.Y.* for *Phil. Nevill*,
at the *Sign of the Gun in Ivy-lane*.
1641.

THE SAINTS SHALL JUDGE THE WORLD, or A REMEDY AGAINST LAWING

As it was delivered in a sermon at the *Courts* held at Northampton, July 9, 1640.

"And I saw seats, and they say upon them, and judgment was given unto them," (Revelation 20:4).

"Such honor have all his saints," (Psalm 149:9).

Introduction:

To the Right Worshipful Sir Christopher Yelverton, Knight (late) High Sheriff of the County of Northampton, all health and happiness.

Sir,

It is the manner of midwives, so soon as the child is born and dressed, to present it first to its own parents, and then to the view of others. This following sermon, as it was first conceived by your motion and request (which is to me a virtual command) so it should first be tendered back to you, that the same party that helped to give it life and bringing forth, might also give it protection and bringing up. The success and operation that it had (as Hercules had with the serpents in his cradle) is to strangle the lawless contentions of this lawing age. I have long and often lamented to see how the entire world is almost turned into one common tribunal, either to sue, or censure others. The great resorts of people in ancient times were accustomed to go to the houses of the prophets for counsel. But now the Inns of Court, and Courts of Justice are more pestered with clients, than the very houses of God. Therefore it is, that for the most part, that profession of the law thrives best of any; and those that, perhaps some of them, envy a 100£ per annum to a painful Levite, with a great deal more ease, themselves get 500£ and think it nothing. The peevish perverseness of men is guilty of this thrift greatly. For if men had either so much grace or wit to do no wrong, or if they do or suffer wrong, to be willing to refer it to their wise and honest brethren, they might have both more peace in their minds, and also more money in their purses. And I cannot but wonder at the forwardness and folly of men, that rather choose to refer it to twelve men in a jury, they who are strangers to him by force and course of the law, than to two men in their neighbors and friends, by the persuasion of the Gospel. In which proceedings, there is this disadvantage at least (besides many more) that where they might have chosen wise and honest arbitrators, their differences fall oftentimes into the hands of many, of which some are wise perhaps, but not honest; others are honest, but no wiser than they should be. In which cases, a good cause, many times, falls to the ground.

To prevent this type of mischief was, as least, one main intention of this sermon. Knowing the weakness of it to walk alone, I have sent forth with it, two of its elder brethren, (two other sermons, preached on other occasions) to wait on it, (and with it on you, Sir) as poor folks used to do, who set the elder to tend on the younger. Such is your noble candor (as I well know) that you will both protect these now made your own, and also lovingly accept what is so duly, so respectfully tendered; not only as a private pledge, but also as a public acknowledgement to the world of my many great engagements for your many undeserved, undesired favors. And I shall never cease (until I cease to be myself) to solicit the Almighty for grace, mercy, and peace on your worthy self, your virtuous lady, and hopeful offspring. Taking it for none of the least favors, that I may profess myself to be,

Yours in all due respects, and service in the Lord.
Daniel Cawdrey.

THE SERMON

"Do you not know, that the saints shall judge the world?" (1 Corinthians 6:2).

The holy Apostle Paul, in the former chapter taxed these Corinthians for their great negligence, in not judging that incestuous person, in an ecclesiastical case. Now, in this chapter he blames them for their *overmuch* diligence in going to judgment in a civil and political matter. He does not inveigh against, much less utterly abolish (as some fanatical Anabaptists dream) the use of secular judgments, which we call *going to law*. He only reprehends the abuses which he observed among them, in the use of that, which in itself (and some cases excepted) might be lawful. "We know, (*to use our Apostle's own words, of another law, the law of God*) the law is good, if a man use it lawfully," (1 Timothy 1:8). Which (at once to confute them, and pass along) we may easily make good, from this very place. For the same Apostle that denies them the use of law, in regard of some circumstances, allows it in regard of others. He denies it in regard of infidels, allows it in regard of the saints, that is, of Christians; as the first verse implies.

But the best thing may be abused; and so is, too often, the law itself. Yet if the abuse may make known the use of a thing, we must pull down the sun out of the firmament. It is true, law and war are much alike. War is but a more public kind of lawing; and law is but a more private kind of warring; and both of them remedies of the last refuge. Yes, on this we will say more, (if that may please and satisfy our secular *antinomians*) that if men were but so wise and honest, as they should be, there would be either none, or little use, either of soldiers or lawyers. If men had but so much honesty, to do no wrong, or so much justice or charity, if they do wrong, to do right (as on the one side, our armor might rust in our houses), so on the other, the courts of justice might have more cobwebs than causes, more spiders than clients. But this may not be expected (do not fear it, O you champions of war, or advocates of either law) while two bitter roots grow in the hearts of men, pride and self-love. The one by which they will do no right; the other, by which they will take no wrong. The best way therefore, that I know, is to consider seriously what are the faults that men usually bring, or rather bring men to those tribunals, and, as much as we can, to labor everyone to redress them. Our Apostle has noted some, and the chiefest, to our hands.

Many were their errors in that proceeding. Some concern the plaintiff, some the defendant, some the spectators.

First, the plaintiff; and what he lacks in weight, he has in number; and they are *five*:

1. *With a brother.* In regard of his adversary; who is noted, nor only generally to be a Corinthian, but to be a Christian. "Dare any of you," you Christian Corinthians. And, "A brother goeth to law with a brother," (verse 6). For an infidel to go to law with an infidel is not strange. For infidel to go to court with a Christian was too common. But Christian with Christian, brother with brother, seems both *unnatural*, and (as those times were) *unchristian*.

2. Before infidels. In regard of the Judge, chosen to decide and umpire their controversies. ἀλλὰ ἀδελφὸς μετὰ ἀδελφοῦ κρίνεται καὶ τοῦτο ἐπὶ ἀπίστων, under the unjust, (verse 6), under the infidels, or unbelievers, and not under the saints. If a brother will go to law with a brother, let them make choice of Christian Judges. For infidels to be judged by Christians, was perhaps not unfit; But for Christians to refuse

Christians, and choose to be judged by infidels, was solely scandalous. What will the heathens say, when Christians are together by the ears, and infidels live in unity?

3. For *trifles*. In regard of the matter, some trifles, of no importance; as in the latter end of this second verse, "Are you unworthy to judge the *least* matters?" Should men fight, that I do not say for Christians, as two cocks for a grain of barley? For a goose in the grass? For a pig in the corner? It is a fault too common, every petty difference pesters these tribunals. Gallio should do well to drive them from the judgment seat, with that word, "I will be no Judge of such matters," (Acts 18:15-16).

4. With impatience. In regard of the matter, with a great deal of impatience and impotent anger. "Why do you not rather take wrong? Why do you not rather suffer yourselves to be defrauded?" (verse 7). Where the Apostle prevents a secret objection. They might plead, "We do not thus proceed without a cause; we have been wronged, perhaps very much, and may we not seek the benefit of the law to right ourselves?" No, the holy Apostle says; something should be hazarded, yes lost, for peace's sake. Christ, your Master,

taught you this lesson, "If any man will take away thy cloak, let him have thy coat also," (Matthew 5). Peace is a jewel, if we knew the worth of it, worth our buying, we would know it is at a dearer rate than most men will give for it. And besides, Saint James has told us the disposition of all truly godly hearts, "The wisdom which is from above, is first pure, then peaceable, gentle, easy to be entreated, full of mercy," (James 3:17). Now truly, there is utterly a fault among you, that you lack that Christian patience, to suffer some wrong, rather than go to law.

5. To *precipitate*. In regard of the order, law should be your *last* refuge, after working through the trials of all other means in vain. Among the rest, reference to your brethren should be used. If they cannot end it, the law is open, implead one another. And this was a principal fault among them, that so soon as any difference arose, they ran or sent presently for a letter of intent to the heathenish courts, and refused to refer it to the saints, as the first verse intimates.

Secondly, there are other faults that concern the defendant; and what he lacks in number, he has in weight.

1. In doing the wrong. That he did the wrong, and so was the occasion or cause of all or most of those errors in the plaintiff, "Nay you do wrong, and defraud, and that your brethren," (verse 8).

2. In defending the wrong done. That he defended wrong done, by denial of satisfaction, to do his brother right; on this he was forced on those scandalous and sinful courses. No, it may seem that he that did the wrong, did not only defend it, but also turned into a plaintiff, (as we call him that begins a suit) and began to sue him first, as the manner of some great ones is; either to vex him, or make him unable to prosecute the former wrong, or to make themselves seem innocent by attending the Apostle's words, "Why do you not rather take wrong?" Which concerns the *plaintiff*, without all question. Yes, (but adds the Apostle) "you do wrong, and defraud;" which, in all congruity, must concern the *defendant*. As if he were both the plaintiff and defendant (a strange mystery) that is, plaintiff in his suit, but defendant of the wrong done, by first complaining. However, there was certainly a fault among them, in one, or other, or both; yes, both, no doubt, are too often to blame. There is utterly a fault that you go to law one with another, ἤδη

μὲν [οὖν] ὅλως ἥττημα ὑμῖν ἐστιν ὅτι κρίματα ἔχετε μεθ' ἑαυτῶν. διὰ τί οὐχὶ μᾶλλον ἀδικεῖσθε; διὰ τί οὐχὶ μᾶλλον ἀποστερεῖσθε; (1 Cor. 6:7), that there are any causes between you, which need the judgment and decision of the law. It is hardly possible to go to law, but that the one party, at least, is faulty.

Thirdly, the spectators, or bystanders, were not altogether innocent. There are two faults to be found in them.

1. Ignorance. Their simplicity or ignorance that they were not able to compromise their brethren's differences, before they went so far, "I speak it to your shame, is it so, that there is not a wise man among you? No, not one, that is able to judge between his brethren? But a brother goeth to law with a brother?" (verse 5). Now verily, there is utterly a fault among you, even you that stand and look on these unkind bickerings, and lack skill to quiet them.

2. Negligence. Their sloth or negligence, that they were so lazy that they would suffer their brethren to go to law, and that under infidels, rather than disease themselves a little, to compose them, being designed by God himself to be Judges of the world. These, I take it, are the principal faults the Apostle

finds with this proceeding of the Corinthians; which being amended, law is, no doubt, lawful, say Anabaptists, what they can to the contrary.

And now we come more near to the words. My text has reference to all the three; but primarily to the plaintiff; and it is brought in as an argument, to dissuade his course, and to disprove his choice. The sum seems to be so much. O Corinthians, O Christians, you are much to blame, that choose such incompetent Judges, of your differences, as infidels are, "Dare any of you, having a matter against another, be judged under the infidels, and not under the saints?" The expostulation is very quick and sharp. If you will necessarily refer your cause to judgment, in all reason, Christians, the saints, were fitter judges than they. Why so? Why, "Do you not know, that the saints shall judge the world?" As if he should say, "If you choose infidels, and refuse Christians, you too much honor the one, and disparage the other. You too much honor infidels in suffering, much more in voluntarily offering yourselves to be judged by them, whom you shall one day judge. You dishonor and disparage Christians, double." First, yourselves, in that you make yourselves inferior to those that shall, one day, be judged by you.

As for example, were it a befitting thing that the honorable judges should refer themselves in any matter of difference, to be judged by the *prisoners* in the jail, whom they shall by and by judge? "Do you not know, that the saints, even you shall judge the world? If then the world shall be judged by you, (as the Apostle argues in the latter part of this verse) is it fit that you should be judged by the world?" Secondly, you disparage your fellow saints, to undervalue them so much as to think infidels worthy of that honor of judicature, rather than them, who shall one day judge the world. As if some persons that have business at this should refuse the honorable bench, and refer themselves to the prisoners, who must be judged by the bench. The argument lies in this way, *a majore ad minus*. If the saints shall judge the world, then, much more, they should judge lesser differences of their brethren, concerning things of this life. That's the latter part of this verse. But certainly the saints shall judge the world, that's the former part of this verse, (for remove the rhetorical interrogation, and it is a strong affirmation) therefore, the *saints* are the fittest judges of Christians' lesser differences. You have the coherence and scope of the words; now take their sum considered absolutely in themselves. They are (if I may be bold to borrow your own terms) a commission granted to the saints; and contain in them two general parts.

1. The dignity itself; *the saints shall judge the world*; and in this, we may consider three things:

1] The commissioners designed, by the name of saints.

2] The matter of the commission, that is, to judge.

3] The latitude, or extent of that commission; the world.

"The saints shall judge the world." What is the certainty of this. "Do you know this?" As if he should say, you do know it, you must know it.

We begin first, with the dignity, and in this, 1. The commissioners deputed, the saints. In which we have two things to consider, the quality of the saints, the one in the sense and signification of the word, the other in the indefiniteness and plurality of the number. We will touch on both.

1. The quality of the saints. The word signifies *Holy*, which is the largest acceptation of it, is equivalent to that of *just*, or *righteous*, as might appear from other places; and must be so taken here, as the opposition in

the former verse evidently manifests. For it is not there opposed to profane, but to the unjust, that is, to infidels or unbelievers, that were generally unjust or unrighteous, as having no true Christian righteousness in them. *Righteousness* in Scripture (and other authors) contains in it not only that particular virtue of justice, but all virtues whatsoever; generally. So unrighteousness does not only parallel that particular virtue of injustice, (from which many heathen judges were set free) but even the lack of all virtues, or most of them. In the 9th and 10th verses of this chapter, laid together, the Apostle explains what he means by the unjust, or unrighteous, "Know you not that the unrighteous shall not inherit the kingdom of God?" The unrighteous, who are they? Mark the next verse. "Neither whoremongers, nor idolaters, *etc.*" Now then, if *unjust* signifies all kinds of unrighteousness, the saints, or *holy ones*, being opposed to them, must likewise *include* all righteousness. The sum is, all God's commissioners for the heavenly judicature must be saints, holy, harmless, innocent, righteous. That is the point. Every man is not fit to be made a judge on earth, much less in heaven. There are three things, we know, that make a complete judge on earth, authority, prudence, and justice, or self-innocence. The first is founded in his commission; and is outside of himself. The other two are within himself, inherent in his person. And if the question is, which of the two is most requisite for a judge? I should venture to say the latter, holiness or innocence, for these *reasons:*

First, justice or holiness makes God himself a competent and complete Judge of the world. So the Scripture often resolves it. "Shall not the Judge of heaven and earth do right?" says Abraham, (Genesis 18:25). "What shall we say then? Is there unrighteousness with God? God forbid. For how shall God then judge the world?" our Apostle says, (Romans 3:5). As if he should say, God himself (with reverence is it spoken) is not a competent Judge, as if he were not perfectly righteous. "The Lord is righteous in all his ways, and holy in all his works." Righteousness and holiness in God are of equal latitude and extent. Now, as God is King of Kings, so he is Judge of Judges, and all his judges must be like himself; Holy as he is holy, and therefore called *King of Saints,* (Revelation 15:3).

Secondly, to avoid reproach and recrimination. If a judge wants for innocence or holiness, he is exposed to contempt, and shall be upbraided with his own errors. "Thou that teachest another, teachest thou not thyself?" (Romans 2:21) was spoken to one of our own. We may enlarge it. You that judge another, do you not judge yourself? You that condemn a man for stealing, do you steal? You that abhor simony, do you commit bribery? *etc.* As that pirate under censure, retorted on the great conqueror, "What I do by sea, thou doest that and more by land, and, many times, great thieves condemn little ones." "Therefore thou art inexcusable O man, whosoever thou art that judgest; for thou that judgest another, condemnest thyself, for thou that judgest doest the same things," or something as bad, (Romans 2:1).

Thirdly, to prevent partiality. For self-guiltiness commonly makes men partial in judging others. Their conscience holds both tongue and hand, and tells them, they do but beat themselves, while they punish others. We may see it in Judah. when his daughter in law Tamar, was accused for her incontinence, how rashly he censures, "Bring her forth, and let her be burned;" but when he heard, "By the man, whose these are, am I with child;" the case is altered, "She is more righteous than I," (Genesis 38) no further talk of burning now; unless he himself will be burned with her. Now on earth, it is too evident that self-iniquity is the mother of all partiality. Therefore, Jehoshaphat giving charge to his judges, to do justly, enforces it from the example of God, whose judges they are. "For (he says) with the Lord, there is no iniquity, nor respect of persons, nor taking of gifts," (2 Chronicles 19:6). As if he should say, "If there is iniquity in the heart, there will be respect of persons, and taking of gifts, to pervert justice. Therefore, it is requisite that they who shall be counted worthy to be judges in heaven, should be saints, privative and men that are like pure gold, purified seven times in the fire, purged from the dross of earthly corruptions; or like pure wine defecated and wracked from the lees and dregs of carnal affections. Such as Chrysippus would have all earthly judges. "Incorrupt, unflatterable, unmerciful and inexorable toward wicked men, terrible in the majesty of equity and truth." Men free from passion and compassion; that will know neither father nor mother, friend nor brother; as was said of Levi in a similar case. For, suppose a judge should meet his child or brother at the bar, and they should entreat, by those near relations, "O my Father, O my brother, *etc.*" What heart not thoroughly hardened, could resist such melting compellations? Perhaps it will be so at the great day of judgment; we have a type of it in the Gospel where our Savior brings in (whether by way of parable, or true history) the rich man beholding Abraham afar off, and Lazarus in his bosom; he dares not speak to Lazarus, who was perhaps a stranger, and was by him before neglected; but to Abraham he addresses himself, with that oily name of Father; "Father Abraham have mercy upon your son." But Abraham was now above relations, above compassions, and foolish pity. "Son remember." So at that great day, there will be crying; "O my father, O my son, O my husband, O my brother!" But there must be judgment without mercy. They, the judges there, must be as insensible and inexorable as Abraham was; and if not pronounce, yet approve and applaud that dreadful sentence on their dearest acquaintance and friends, "Go ye cursed into everlasting fire." What manner of men then ought they to be, that must be judges of the world, in, "all holiness and godliness," (2 Peter 3:11) (so the Apostle's words are) that is in the perfection of holiness and godliness; "perfecting holiness in the fear of God," (2 Corinthians 7:1) as our Apostle speaks. To conclude this first point; however on earth, though favor or affection, bribery or corruption, may sometime be made to judge; as that Roman could say, to his little credit, "With a great sum of money, obtained I this office," (Acts 22:28). Yet in heaven none but saints shall judge the world, and that's the first. The second follows.

2. Their equality; *Sancti*, in the plural, and indefinitely, the saints. And I do not fear to say, in the words of the Psalmist, "Such honor have all his saints," (Psalm 149:9). They are fellow-commissioners; If I do not mistake, all our judges are so; and so are all our justices at the quarter sessions; one commission includes them all. There are indeed distinct altitudes, in respect of their personal titles, and degrees, but no different latitudes, in respect of their commission; in this they are all equal. Heaven observes the same proportion. One star differs from another in glory, not in nature. The least is as true a star, as those of the greatest magnitude. One saint differs from another, perhaps, in personal glory in heaven, as I personal grace on earth; but the meanest, the lowest, is as truly a saint, as the greatest, and as truly a commissioner and judge of the world. There may and must be difference of order and priority, to avoid confusion, but no disparity of dignity in this heavenly judicature. Our Savior tells his

disciples so. "You shall sit upon twelve thrones, judging the twelve tribes of Israel," (Matthew 19:28). They all have thrones, all sit, all judge; Matthias the last, as well as Peter the first. What? Only twelve Apostles? Shall none sit upon thrones and judge but they? What shall then become of Paul, and other saints? He that made the question, can best resolve it, Saint Augustine, "We ought not to think (he says) that only those twelve men shall judge with Christ; for by that number is signified the whole multitude of judges. Otherwise the Apostle Paul, who labored more than all of them, shall lack a room to sit on; who yet demonstrates, that himself with other saints, do belong to that number, when he says, *Do you not know that the saints shall judge the world?* And again in the next verse, *Know you not that we shall judge angels?*" The Catholic schoolmen (falsely so called) some of them here are not Catholic enough. They restrain this dignity only to the Apostles, and such as have followed them, by profession of vowed poverty, to the honor of their recluses and monastic superstition. Their color is slight, and vanishing. Because (*forsooth*) our Savior, answering Peter's question, "Master we have forsaken all, and what shall we have?" it says, "You shall sit upon twelve thrones, and judge." But the Apostle

Paul, who had the mind of Christ, and the Spirit of God, and had been once in heaven, has enlarged the commission to all saints, even to these poor Corinthians, the most despised, and least esteemed among them. And therefore it is observable how he varies the person, and makes use of all the persons in the plural number; *We, you, they*. Not only, "We shall judge the angels," (verse 3) which might be applied to the Apostles, and no other; nor only, "*You* shall judge the world," or "The world shall be judged by you," which might exclude others, besides the Corinthians; but, "*The saints* shall judge the world," in the words of our text. *We shall judge, you shall judge, all saints shall judge the world.* But Saint Jude makes it utterly clear by the ancient testimony of Enoch, the seventh from Adam. "Behold the Lord cometh with thousands of his saints, to execute judgment upon all the ungodly," (verse 14) which Daniel reckons to be thousand thousands, and ten thousand times ten thousand, even *all* his saints. Even to the least of all God's saints, is this honor given; how poorly, how basely he is esteemed of in this world, he shall be in commission to judge the world. They went about, some of them, in sheepskins and goatskins, (not like judges in scarlet) and yet, of them the world was not worthy, though they are accounted worthy to judge the world, (Hebrews 11). The Romans fetched some from the plough, to the dictatorship. Pharaoh took Joseph out of prison, to be the second in Egypt. David was sent for, from the sheepfolds, to be anointed with regal oil, "As he was following the ewes (good shepherd) he took him, that he might feed Jacob his people, and Israel his inheritance," (Psalm 78:71-72). This is sure, God fetches his saints further, even from the lowest earth, to the highest heavens. "He raiseth up the poor out of the dust, and lifteth up the needy out of the dunghill; That he may set him with princes, even with the Prince of his people; Such honor have all his saints," (Psalm 113:6). And now I have finished with the first part of the three named, and pass on to the second main point.

2. The commission granted, or matter of the commission, "The saints shall judge." There are, by Kings, several commissions granted, not all alike honorable; Some, for matters of *Nisi Prius*, as you call them; and perhaps many more, which I do not know, nor care much to learn. That is the most eminent, which you call, "A Commission of *Oyer* and *Terminer*," which passes upon life and death; because it concerns

that which is most dear and precious in man, his life. God's preferments are ever like himself, most gracious, most glorious, to the best and highest employments. If there is any commission weightier, either in honor or execution, that shall be conferred upon his saints. "Do you know, that the saints shall judge?" and that with the judgment of condemnation? For explication of it, two things are to be inquired; first, the truth, and then the time; the one in the sense of the word, *judge*; the other in the sense of the very, *shall judge*. We follow both.

1. First, we grant that the truth of this may well be scrupled; *How the saints can be said to judge*. Seeing first, we have God himself, (as well he may) taking this honor to himself, "God is Judge himself," (Psalm 50:6). Secondly, granting a general and universal commission to his Son, "The Father hath committed all judgment to the Son, even as," or "because he is the Son of man," (John 5:32). And thirdly, we have the Son discharging all from this employment, "Judge not, that you not be judged," (Matthew 7:1). And yet here Saint Paul tells us of a commission of judgment, granted to the saints. For reconciliation of this, we must distinguish of judgment and judges.

1) Of judgment; which, for kind or manner, is manifold; as may appear in these particulars.

1] There is *Judicium Authoritatis*. The judgment of authority; which resides in the king, as root and fountain; and thus there is only one Judge of the world, as one Lawgiver, God is Judge himself.

2] *Judicium Declarationis*, by way of declaration; and thus the book of the laws and statutes may be said to judge, because they declare who, and how men are to be judged. And indeed, it is the law that judges, not the Judge; he pronounces the judgment of the law. So said they of old, "We have a law, and by our law he ought to die. Doth our law condemn a man, before it hear him speak?" said another. And thus, the Word of God, the book of the law, is said to judge. "The Word that I have spoken, shall judge you at the last day," (John 12:48); said our Savior.

3] *Judicium Prolationis*, by way of pronunciation, or passing of the sentence. And this is done by the Judge alone, as our experience tells us. And in this sense, Christ, as man, shall judge alone; "All judgment is committed unto him;" and he shall pronounce that dreadful sentence, "Go you cursed," passing the final doom upon the world.

4] *Judicium Corporationis*; by way of comparison, and thus not only the saints, but one wicked man shall judge and condemn another. So our Savior tells some; "Tyre and Sidon shall rise in judgment with this generation, and condemn it." And thus the saints, not only *shall*, but even *now* judge the world. Their lives are *a living law*; their examples of holiness, in the same temptations with other men, shall rise up and condemn the world that did not follow their patterns in the same allowance of means.

5] *Assessionis & Approbationis* (for I join them both together) by way of *Assession* and *Approbation*; as the Justices on the bench sit together with the Judge, and approve his judgment. And so, especially, all the saints shall judge the world; *They shall sit upon seats or thrones, and approve,* yes, *applaud the sentence.* "The righteous shall rejoice, when he sees the vengeance."

2) Of Judges, we may also distinguish; whereof there are several kinds, in a well settled state.

1] The King is the supreme Judge of all, within his own dominions, and God is Judge of the entire world, by way of authority.

2] The Lord Chancellor is a general deputed Judge, by delegation from the King himself judges no man. So Christ, made the Great Lord Chancellor, or Lord Chief Justice of all the world, "The Father judgeth no man, but hath committed all judgment to the Son."

3] The twelve Judges are for their private courts, or particular circuits. And thus we may (perhaps) grant, the twelve Apostles, by special privilege, shall judge the twelve tribes of Israel.

4] All the Justices at their quarter sessions are joint-commissioners; And thus again the saints, even all the saints shall judge, in the manner aforesaid.

I conclude this point with that of Saint Peter, with a little alteration. Seeing these things are this way, "What manner of persons ought they to be, in all manner of holy conversations and godliness, looking for and hasting unto the coming of the Day of the Lord," (2 Peter 3:11-12), when the saints shall judge the world. For the time is not yet, but shall shortly come, when the saints shall judge; And that's the second thing observed.

2. The time, or date of this commission; It is not, *do judge*, for that is expressly forbidden, "Judge not," but, "shall judge." It does not bear date until the Great Day of Judgment arises, at the end of the world. It was the speech of him, who is Lord of the saints, yes, King of

saints, when he was in this world, "I came not to judge the world, but to save it," (John 12:47). It is enough for the saints to be like their Lord and Master; He did not come to judge, but to be judged; but "he ascended into heaven and from thence he shall come to judge the quick and the dead," says our Creed. "God hath appointed a Day, wherein he will judge the world, by that Man, whom he hath appointed," (Acts 17:31). He shall come openly among the just, to judge justly, who came secretly to be judged by the unjust, unjustly. He shall sit as Judge, who stood before a Judge. *He shall condemn the truly guilty, who was falsely accounted guilty*; as elegantly Saint Augustine says. Even as he was, so are his saints in this world. They judge no man, their hour has not yet come. They are judged of all men, for this is the hour and the day of the world's judgment. As thieves and malefactors in the jail sometimes in mockery will represent the delusion of innocence, and there cite, arraign, accuse, condemn their Judges. So wicked men deal with God's saints, in this world, in the same way. But the Day of Judgment will come when the Judges shall in earnest condemn those malefactors, who thus spotted themselves with their own destruction. The saints shall judge, but not yet. And there are good reasons of this prorogation.

1) Their ignorance, and lack of experience. There are many difficult and perplexed cases, which, what by reason of the subtlety of wicked men, and what by the secrecy of the intentions of men's hearts, they are not able to determine, without danger of error. It was an intricate business propounded to young Solomon, that of the two harlots, to find out the true mother of the child, when no evidence could appear on either side. And therefore it is said, "The wisdom of God was in him to do justice," (1 Kings 3:18). I have read of a case sometime propounded to the Areopagites, judges among the Athenians, which, because they could not well assail, they wisely commanded the parties to come again a hundred years after, and they would do them justice. By that time, they thought, either they, the Judges, or the parties would be dead. To this purpose, may that of the Apostle be fitly applied; "Judge nothing before the time, until the Lord come, who both will bring to light the hidden thing of darkness, and will make manifest the counsels of the hearts."

2) Their impotence, in regard of their affections; they are too much subject to passion and compassion. Fear, love, hatred, foolish pity, are able to corrupt the best judgment. Our friends may persuade us, our enemies may provoke us; the one to be too favorable, the other to be too harsh and cruel. I have read another story fitting to this purpose. "In China, a part of the Indies, no man may rule, or bear any office of justice in the town, or place, where he was born; lest his parents, or other friends, should work him to give sentence of judgment, contrary to the rules of equity." And, I take it, it is the custom of this our nation, that no judge rides circuit to that country where he dwells, perhaps, for the very same reason. However, this we know. This world is the hometown of our nativity; we live here among our friends, among our enemies, who are many times, (too often, only God knows) the snares of justice. Therefore, our God thinks it fit to remove us from our native soul, before he employs us in that state-business of judgment. I conclude this point, let the censorious world spend itself in judging and condemning the saints; it is but man's day, as the Apostle calls it, (1 Corinthians 4:3) but man's judgment, that may, and must be repealed. There will

come the Day of the Lord, as the Day of Judgment is called, (2 Peter 3:10); yes, the Day of the saints will come; and then the course of things shall be clean altered. The world now judges the saints, then the saints shall judge the world; and that is the next and last part.

3. The extent or latitude of the commission, *the world*. As Kings' commissions differ in their subject matter, so also in their extent; some are for one town or city; some for one or more counties, the largest is but for their kingdom. It is said of Samuel, "That he went from year to year in circuit to Bethel, and Gilgal, and Mizpah, and judged Israel in all those places," (1 Samuel 7:16, 1 Chronicles 19:5). But afterwards this was divided among many Judges, as we may see in the time of Jehoshaphat. Yet, what if a man's commission reached over the whole kingdom; what is that to the whole world, but a molehill to a mountain? If further (which never yet was granted to one man) over the whole world, for one generation, what is that to the innumerable generations past and to come? Which yet are all subject to the judgment of the saints. "Know you not that the saints shall judge the world?" The world has diverse acceptations in Scriptures. Here it is taken

for the worse part, the wicked men of the world, the unjust, in the first verse, the infidels in the sixth verse, as opposed to the saints; not excluding, but rather including the wicked angels, that is, the devils. The Apostle adds in the next verse, "Know you not that we shall judge angels?" The argument rises by way of gradation, the saints may well be allowed to judge your lesser matters of this life; for in the life to come, they shall judge the world of wicked men, nay more, they shall judge the wicked angels. "Such honor have all God's saints." Not to make too much of this, but, why might not Christ himself alone judge them, and no more ado? Why shall the saints judge both men and angels? For three *reasons*:

1) To the greater torment and vexation of wicked men, and devils, when they shall see those very men whom they scorned, oppressed, persecuted, to be now advanced, not only to glory, but to be their Judges. Those angels, who sometime disdained to be servants to man, (as some think) that tempted, seduced, vexed man, shall now, to their further torment, see them gloriously advanced to be their Judges. Those wicked men who said, as they to Lot with much disdain, "He came in as a stranger, and shall he rule us? Shall be

moved, not more with grief, than torment of indignation, to see them thus exalted over them." and that so much more, as they more esteemed them base and inferior. To find themselves delivered over into the hands of their enemies, to be judged, of whom they can expect no mercy, what horror must it needs breed in them? As if, when some noble man or judge, had wronged some poor and mean man, the King should deliver him over into the power of that man, to take his own revenge. As Abraham did to Hagar, to Sarah; and Joshua did to those heathen kings to every common soldier, to set his feet upon their necks. "God shall tread Satan under your feet shortly," is promised to the *saints*. To this purpose is that of the Psalmist, speaking of the great advancement of the righteous, "The ungodly shall see this, and be grieved, he shall gnash with his teeth (for indignation) and melt away," (Psalm 112:10). So our Savior tells those auditors of his, "There shall be weeping and gnashing of teeth, when you shall see Abraham, and Isaac, and Jacob, in the Kingdom of heaven, and yourselves thrust out," (Luke 13:27-28). Hell itself would not be a perfect hell, if the wicked should not know and see the saints, whom they have abused, to be glorious.

2) For their own greater assurance and security. They shall be their own judges; if they are favorable, it is their own fault. They shall not only see a just retribution on their enemies, on both men and devils, but have their own voice, and hand in its execution. They shall not anymore need to fear the persecutions of wicked men, or the wearying solicitations of wicked angels. All their enemies shall be destroyed, and for their greater security, "When the ungodly shall perish, they shall see it with their eyes," (Psalm 9:18), and help to act it with their own hand. There shall be a mutual view of each other, in heaven, and hell. When the righteous are exalted, the ungodly shall see it. As the ungodly perish and are tortured into eternity, the righteous shall see it. Dives[2] as well sees Lazarus in Abraham's bosom, as Lazarus sees Dives in hell, and a gulf is set between, that they can never come near one another, either to comfort, or hurt one another anymore.

3. For their greater joy. We used to take wonderful contentment and pleasure in the misery and destruction of those whom we esteem our enemies (though (Proverbs 24:17-18) sinfully sometimes, I

---

[2] *Dives* is the Latin name of the Rich Man in hell.

confess, on earth) much more, if we may have liberty to revenge ourselves on them. "The righteous shall rejoice, when he seeth the vengeance, he shall wash his footsteps in the blood of the ungodly," (Psalm 58:10) the Psalmist says, and that without the least sin, in heaven; where God himself, shall laugh and mock at the just condemnation of wicked and ungodly men. I conclude all this first part with that speech of the sweet singer of Israel, which, I think, was spoken by way of prophecy, of this very day of the saints' judgment. "Let the saints be joyful in glory, let them sing aloud upon their beds. Let the high praises of God be in their mouths, and a two-edged sword in their hands. To execute vengeance upon the heathen, and punishments upon the people. To bind their kings in chains, and their princes in fetters of iron. To execute upon them the vengeance, as it is written, Such honor have all his saints," (Psalm 149:5-9). Do you not know that the saints shall judge the world?

And now we come to the second general part of the text, the certainty of this dignity of the saints. Do you not know it? It fares with God's saints here, as with men's heirs in their minority. Though they are lords of all, yet many years pass, before they know their inheritance, or the privileges and honors of it. God has provided more for his saints than they do know, than they can know. But yet, this they do know, or must know, that the saints, even they themselves shall judge the world. The rhetoric shows the divinity; the interrogation negative makes it strongly affirmative. You may know it, you do know it, you must know it; for it is the most useful and necessary that *all* know it. And so I will now make the application of all that has been spoken in the former part by way of explication; which, of purpose, I have reserved for the conclusion. It is therefore very profitable for all parts that it should be known. Some things concern the world, some the saints, and some both.

1. The world (we begin with them). Let all wicked men know it, if they do not know it already, that the saints, whom they now scorn and wrong, shall one day be their Judges. *Then:*

1] Let them take heed how they sin before the saints. They shall be their Judges, and dare they make them their witnesses? That these men are quite bold, these who dare scorn such people in the face and view of the Judge. A good consideration, if men were not thinking past what they should in their minds, as well as receiving grace, to restrain the impudent looseness of profane men. If they do not fear God, whom they cannot see, and therefore do not believe that he sees them, yet, let them revere men, who do see them, and whom they see. The presence of some great senator has this power, in a tumultuous multitude, when those outrageous citizens saw the chief captain, they left beating Paul. Sanctity should make impurity blush, if it were not grown bloodless. Herod feared John the Baptist, because he was a saint, a just man, (Acts 21:32); what if he had known he should one day be his Judge? When Paul was but reasoning of righteousness, temperance, and the judgment to come, Felix trembled, (Acts 24). Yet little did he think his Judge was right there. They are worse than Herod or Felix, who neither fear nor tremble to sin before the saints, who yet would be thought to know and believe this Scripture, "That the saints shall judge the world."

2] Let them at least take heed, how they wrong and abuse the saints. The saints shall be their judges, and dare they make them also their accusers? "He reproved even Kings for their sakes, saying, Touch not mine anointed, and do my prophets no harm." If the malefactor was not mad or desperate, that would anger his Judge, and offer him injury, in words or deeds, as he was coming to the bar, or going towards the Judgment seat? What hope did he have of any favor? Dives did not dare speak a word to Lazarus (as we noted before) whom he had but neglected, but entreats his Father Abraham for mercy. Hear it, all wicked oppressors, slanderers, persecutioners of God's saints, you had as good, no *better*, abuse one of his Majesty's Judges, as wrong any, the poorest, the meanest of God's saints. You have abused a Judge, yes your own Judge. Take it for good counsel, if you will not be good yourselves, yet do not hurt those that are good. No, do not hurt. Yes, make them your friends (as men do the Judges) by your unrighteous mammon, when a friend in the court will be worth more than all the money in your purses. At least, I say, do not wrong them, for certainly they must be your Judges. Agree with your adversary quickly while you are in the way with him. Unless your adversary deliver you to the Judge, who is wholesome in his counsel. I say more, let your adversary prove to be your Judge. For now you know that the saints shall judge the world. And so much for the *world*.

2. The saints. Let them take notice of this certain truth, his excellent privilege; that they shall judge the world. It *serves:*

1] For a ground, not only of comfort against those hard pressures, and great dejection, to which they are subjected in this world, but also of patience, in the censures and judgments of the world, as those that know their turn and time of judgment is coming. See how confidently the apostle condemns the censures of men, "With me it is a small matter, that I should be judged of you, or of man's judgment," (1 Corinthians 4:3) as the original text has it. "Let the same mind be in you, that was in Christ Jesus, who humbled himself to the death, even the death of the cross," (Philippians 2:5, 8); not only to be judged, but to die. Or as the Apostle Saint Peter expresses it, "Christ suffered for us, leaving us an example, that we should follow his steps," (2 Peter 2:21). He suffered to be censured, reviled, mocked, crucified; but he shall come to judge both the quick and the dead. "When Christ, which is our life shall appear, then shall you also appear with him in glory," (Colossians 3:4) our Apostle says. "Behold the Lord cometh with thousands of his saints, to execute judgment," says Saint Jude. "Be patient (and comfortable) therefore brethren (they are Saint James' words) "Behold the Judge stands before the door," (James 5:7).

2] For a caveat against the company of the wicked world; the saints shall be their judges, and do they now make them their companions? Have no fellowship with the unfruitful works of darkness, but reprove them rather. How? By abstaining from their company, which is a real reproof, and a previous condemnation; *Prajudicium aterni judicii*, as that Father in a similar case, the prejudgment of that eternal judgment. How often are they called on for this? "What fellowship hath light with darkness? God with Belial?" "What commerce or society have Judges that must condemn, with malefactors, who are to be condemned," asks Tertullian. Know yourselves (O you who profess yourselves saints) know your worth and dignity, with God. He purposes to make you his Judges of the world, and do you make yourselves equal to the world? "Come out from among them, and touch no unclean thing." Avoid their company, abandon their fellowship, as well as their fashions. Do not be partakers of their sins, or enter communion with them, lest you be partakers of their punishments. "For (so adds Tertullian) unless we now prejudge and precondemn in them those things, for which we shall then judge and condemn them, certainly they shall judge and condemn us." Let the saints consider it.

3] For a strong argument and motive to peacemaking on all hands. And this is indeed the principal scope of the Apostle; where it is worth the while to consider, the admirable wisdom of the Apostle, in making one argument infer a double conclusion. This is one in regard of the parties at variance, the other in regard of the spectators that suffered them to go to law. For mark the words. In the first verse, he gives a sharp increpation[3] to the parties going to law, "Dare any of you (either plaintiff or defendant) having a matter against another, go to law before the unjust, and not before the saints?" *Why not?* some man might say. Why, do you not know, the saints shall judge the world? How much more, lesser matters, but then, lest those that were beholders should applaud themselves as innocent, mark how he changes the words in the latter part of the verse, "If then the world shall be judged by you, are you unworthy to judge the smallest matters?" which cannot, in any

---

[3] *Increpation*, a rebuke or reproof.

reasonable construction, be referred to the parties at variance, (it being utterly unfit that men should be their own Judges) therefore he secretly taxes those that were bystanders, for not interrupting their proceedings by a wise and timely arbitrament; on the same ground still, "Do you not know that the saints, even you, shall judge the world?" We will apply it severally, first to the parties, then to the spectators.

1) To the litigant parties, or contending, whether plaintiff or defendant, it does not matter. The Apostle would have neither of them go to law, at least before or under unbelievers. No, he would have neither of them go to law at all (as Saint Chrysostom does not observe amiss) if the matter might, by and a fair means, be ended by the saints. For he does principally blame them, not so much for going to law before infidels, as for not referring their matters to a private decision. He does not oppose Christian tribunals, to the tribunals of infidels, but public lawing to private determination. My reasons are, first, there were no Christian magistrates in those times of the Church, but all were heathenish, and therefore he could not refer them to such as were not. Secondly, in Greek, the word does not only signify a public sentence, but oftentimes a

private censure, as many instances would confirm, if we could stand upon it. I get to the point then. The parties at variance must not go to law, until their brethren cannot end it. They must first refer it to their fellow saints. This the Apostle urges on them, by this argument, "Do you not know," as if he should say, "Are the saints so highly honored by God, to be made Judges of the world, and do you think them unworthy to compose your lesser differences?" There is therefore utterly a fault among you, that you thus disparage the commissioners of heaven, the saints; and not expose yourselves only, by your profession also, and the professor of the Gospel, to the scorn and derision of the infidels. For what will the heathen say? See how injurious, how malicious, how contentious these Christians are! Not a man among them that has so much judgment or wisdom, as to determine the least difference that arises, but they must come to us for judgment. We cannot, in our land (blessed be God) make that a difference of infidel and Christian. But yet we have a distinction parallel to that of papists and protestants; atheists and truly religious. And this was the sufficient argument to a good heart, not to bring his differences into the public eye of the world, until he had tried all other means in vain. For what will papists say? As of our Church differences, they say, "These are your Protestants; *ut se invicem diligunt!* See how they low, or rather hate and prosecute one another!" What will atheists and profane persons say? "These are your professors, these are those that would be called saints, (as in the text) see how they fight, and war, and devour one another! See how simple and weak they are, that there is not a wise man among them, to judge between his brethren!" Why then, O why should Christians so disparage one another, to think them unable or unworthy to judge their lesser matters, who are so far honored by God, to be Judges of the world. And perhaps, when all is done, the business falls into the hands of some, who are neither wise nor honest; who are of the world, and must one day be judged by the saints? Let not, O let not then either papists or atheists, I say not, be Judges, but nor spectators, nor witnesses of these unkind and unchristian quarrels. Refer them, refer them to your brethren, and smother them in the first smoking. "Do you not," both parties, "know that the saints shall judge the world?"

  2) To the spectators. The Apostle would have them both wise and willing to undertake, if not the

prevention, yet the speedy conclusion of such differences between their brethren. And the argument is strong for them. "Do you not know, *etc.*" "If then the world shall be judged by you, are you unworthy to judge the smallest matters?" Truly, my brethren the dishonor is greater than you are aware of. If you are willing, but unable, it is your shame. "I speak it to your shame, (our Apostle says) Is it so, that there is not a wise man among you, no not one, that is able to judge between his brother? But a brother goes to law with a brother?" If you are able, but unwilling, it is your blame, even want of a great deal of piety to God, and charity to your brethren. How can you think yourselves able or worthy (willing I know you will be) to judge the world, that lack either skill or will, to judge between your brethren? Be admonished then, (I speak it, I hope, in a good time, to prevent many public differences hereafter, though I expect no fee for my counsel) be admonished, I say, every man, to spend some time, some labor, some pains, to repair the first breaches of your brethren's peace. Entreat them, beseech them, adjure them, for their own sake, for peace's sake, for religion's sake, for God's sake, to yield to a private determination. I conclude things here. If defendant, spectators, labor to repair it. Live in peace, and the God of love and peace shall be with you. So we have covered this particular in reference to the saints.

3. To both saints and the world as being mixed together; and we have two things to propound to *them:*

1] Moderation of their censures, in judging one another; How often, how earnestly are we called upon to this purpose? "Judge not, that you be not judged," (Matthew 7:1) says our Lord and Master. "Judge nothing before the time," Saint Paul says. What expostulations the same Apostle makes in excess in this particular point? "Who art thou, that judgest another man's servant? Why dost thou judge thy brother? And why dost thou set at naught thy brother?" (Romans 14:4, 10). Why do you *vilify*, or as Tertullian expresses the sense of that word, why do you *nullify* your brother? Yet as if the Day of Judgment had come already, we are all Judges one of another. It is a world of wonder to see how the world is made one common tribunal, where every man ascends the throne, or place of judgment, and there are arraigns, accusations, and condemnations to his brother.

At least we keep our turns. Now we judge others; then others get up and judge us, as if we all were judges, and all delinquents. Among ourselves, we may divide all into two classes, profane and religions, but both agree, or rather, disagree in more strict and precise than themselves, mad, foolish, simple, superstitious, in a word (the worst they can say) hypocrites. On the other side, those that are strictly and would be thought truly religious, discharge as fast as them; Papists, atheists, profane, wicked; yes (which I tremble to think on) reprobates. O Lord! where will our indiscreet zeal and impetuous rashness carry us? O men and brethren forbear, forbear. Who made you Judges in this world? When your Savior would not be a Judge in a case of *Nisi prius*, to divide an inheritance, but refused it, on this very reason, "Man, who made me a Judge or a divider betwixt you," (Luke 12:14); how dare you to be so bold, as to judge of life and death, and that eternal, of the soul? Suppose you shall be Judges of the world, yet not in this world. Will you anticipate and antidate your commission? Wicked men are mere usurpers; they are to be judged, not to judge at all. The saints are too precipitate to start up into the judgment seat, (as Absalom into his Father's throne before his death) before the time. I say to both, Do not judge now, that you are not judged for your labor. "Speak not evil one of another, brethren; he that speaketh evil of his brother and judgeth his brother, speaketh evil of the law, and judgeth the law, but if you judge or condemn the law, thou art not a doer of the law, but a Judge," (James 4:11). They are Saint James' words, and not mine. Saint Paul shall close up this point. "Judge nothing before the time, till the Lord come;" until the Day of Judgment.

2] A strong enforcement for holiness, that thus qualifies a man to make him a Judge of the world. The Apostle shall speak what I intend, fully to my foregoing discourse, "Follow peace with all men, (hear it plaintiff, defendant, and spectators) and holiness, (hear it all men) without which no man shall see the Lord," (Hebrews 12:14), without which, no man shall ever be a Judge in heaven, whatever he be on earth. Labor above all things for holiness, they that want it, to procure it; they that have it, to increase it; "Do you not know, that the saints," that is, the holy ones, and they only, "shall judge the world?" "O! you sons of men, how long will you have such pleasure in vanity, and seek after lies? Know you that the Lord hath chosen to himself the man that is godly," (Psalm 4) the man that is holy, to make a Judge of in heaven. How long, O! you profane ones, you scoffers and deriders of Holiness, will you despise and scorn that which must be your Judge? Kings choose Judges chiefly for their knowledge and experience; God chooses his by conscience and holiness. If these two must be severed, God says, Let me have the man that has more conscience and less science; rather than him, that has all science and no conscience. Come then, my brethren, come to the Inns of Court, these courts of God's houses, and study holiness, more than knowledge, that you may be accounted worthy to be made Judges of the world. Knowledge without holiness may make a man a Judge indeed, but not of the world, but of himself. Such a man is *self-judged*, self-condemned, to save the Judges a labor. Holiness is the very seal of our commission; or at least the *posie* written round about it, holiness to the Lord, as the Prophet in a similar case, (Zechariah 14:20). The Apostle tells us so. "The foundation of God stands sure, and hath this seal, the Lord knoweth who are his," but that is the privy seal. The broad seal is that which follows, "Let every one that calls upon the name of the Lord, depart from iniquity," (2 Timothy 2:19); that is, let him be holy. If any man pretends to have a commission for this judicature, and it lacks this inscription, it is a counterfeit, and merely forged. This holiness is the thing which God esteems above all things in his Judges; and which, above all things, as we said at first, makes God himself a competent Judge of the world. And thus he requires and expects his Judges should be qualified with it, above all his other attributes. Not that they should be like him, in power, wisdom, *etc.* but in holiness. "Be you holy as I am holy. Be perfect, as your heavenly Father is perfect," (2 Corinthians 1:26). No (if we may, as we may, believe Saint Paul), "Not many wise, not many noble, not many mighty are called," out to this preferment. "But God hath chosen the foolish things of the world, to confound the wise. and the weak things of the world to confound the things that are mighty. and base things of the world, and things that are despised, hath God chosen," to make his Judges of. You should covet the best thing then and that is holiness. Let others scoff at holiness. Let others be ambitious for honor, for knowledge, for wealth, for pleasure; but, if you will hear my counsel and advice, be covetous, ambitious, zealous for *holiness*. One grain of true holiness shall advance you higher with God in heaven, than a whole world of greatness without it. When I have prayed for you in the Apostle's words, I shall have done, and be no further tedious. "Now the very God of peace, sanctify you throughout, and I pray God, that your whole spirits, souls and bodies, may be kept blameless, till the coming of our Lord Jesus Christ" (1 Thessalonians 5:23); that is, until the Day of Judgment, the great and grand court and then you shall see the difference between the righteous and the wicked, between him that serves God, and him that does not serve him; between the holy and profane. Then shall it manifest to the entire world, that the saints, and the saints only, shall judge the world. Now to the King of saints, the Holy, Holy, Holy God, be ascribed of us, and of all his saints, as is most due, all holiness and honor, all might and majesty, all power and glory, from henceforth and forever. *Amen.*

A CLOSE HYPOCRITE DISCOVERED

"Love rejoiceth not in iniquity, but rejoiceth together with the truth," (1 Corinthians 13:6).

"God, I thank thee, that I am not as other men are, extortioners, unjust, adulterers, or even as this publican," (Luke 18:11).

1. The coherence. It does not matter so much sometimes what, as *with what* mind men speak. When Judas was sad, concerning the ointment poured upon our Savior's head, "What means all this waste? This ointment might have been sold, and given to the poor," (John 12:5-6); the words were seemingly very charitable, but the mind was nothing less, in the judgment of the Evangelist, who knew him better than we. "This he spake, not because he cared for the poor, but because he was a thief." The text we are considering is very similar to this, and is observable in this present speech of the Pharisee. For whom, in a mere looking at the words in the text, without respect to his mind and intention that spoke it, would not take

him, not only for a good and honest, but also for a very pious and devout man. He seems to be, 1. So thankful, and 2. Thankful for such a mercy, as few men take notice of, or acknowledge any favor, viz. that he is not so bad as other men. Many indeed (being more sensible of corporal, then spiritual mercies) seem thankful that they are not so miserable, sick, poor, and as other men; but few, beside this Pharisee (or those that are truly godly) give thanks to God, they are not so *bad* or sinful as other men. But he that knew the heart better than we hear these words, has discovered that which we do not dare have censured, that this so glorious seeming of a sentence proceeded from a deep and gross *hypocrisy*. For both the Evangelist, in his preface to the parable, did not tell us his aim and end; partly to justify himself, and partly to vilify others, with proud scorning and despising of them, "He spake this parable to certain that trusted in themselves, that they were righteous, and despised others:" And also our blessed Savior, the parable Maker, has informed us of the issue (no doubt answerable to his intention) that God rejected this pretended thankfulness. The poor publican went away justified, not the Pharisee.

2. The division. The words then (you see) may two ways be considered. Either, absolutely in themselves; and so they are very good, and beside other good things in them, this is not the least, that he is thankful (or at least thought he ought to be thankful) for this privative or negative mercy, that he was *not so bad as other men*. Or else respectively, with regard to the man, or his mind that spoke them, and so they are very bad; as bad almost as can be, even an intimation of a kind of diabolical rejoicing at others' badness; as if he would thank God, there was scarcely an honest man in the world except for himself. In this he was taking a kind of complacency and contentment in their illness, for ends after this to be specified. Saint Paul indeed has a speech something like this, but with a great deal of difference in the intention of the speaker, when he writes in this way to his Romans, "God be thanked, that ye were the servants of sin; but ye have obeyed from the heart the form of doctrine to which ye were delivered," (Romans 6:17). He does not give God thanks, that they were impious for the Apostle to do, or us to think, but that having been the servants of sin, they had now obeyed the form of doctrine delivered to them. Had this Pharisee thanked God, that he was

better than other men; or not so bad as other men, with a simple and humble mind, he had been worthy to be commended; but when as he does this with a proud and scornful mind, he seems to be glad, and pleased, that others *were* so bad, and so *much worse* than himself. And this we may observe, that we well cannot (or seldom do) give thanks for that, in which we do not somewhat take joy, and take delight. Little joy makes cold thanks; but as thankfulness increases joy, so joy produces thankfulness. Now, that a man should spend his joy or thanks for others' badness, is a wickedness incident to none but devilish dispositions; and this, we think, was justly taxable in this Pharisee.

3. The observation confirmed. To handle the words in both of these respects, the time will not permit; we will therefore look upon them in the second consideration, with respect to the mind of the speaker, as it is discovered to us; and occasionally take in such points of the former, as do, or may pertain to the application of the latter. The point of observation will be this: *That whatever shows of goodness a hypocrite may make, yet he is secretly glad, and takes delight in others' badness.* "God, I thank thee, I am not as other men are," which is a kind of triumph or insult over other men's infirmities, and

especially over the poor publican, who was reputed one of the chief sinners of those times, and most odious and infamous. Now, had the Pharisee only looked at his own credit (as no doubt in part he did look at) he would not have compared himself with men so notoriously bad. For what honor or excellence is it for a man not to be so naught as a publican? Especially for a Pharisee, whose profession was most eminent in those times? It would have been better in such an intention, to have left out this clause, and to have told of his own extraordinary perfections, as after he does, "I fast twice in the week, I give tithes of all I do possess." But making such a comparison, in such a manner, discovers a naughty disposition of a soul, that it pleased itself with others' badness, or being worse than himself. This corruption of heart is more grossly manifested by some, who openly make themselves merry with other men's infirmities. The fool counts it a sport to commit wickedness, (Proverbs 10:23); not only himself, but to see others do so too; as to hear men swear, or curse, or fret. A hypocrite does the same, though more closely; he seems to thank God, that he is not so bad as others, when indeed he is glad others are not so good as he. The contrary of this appears in those that are truly good, as they desire others' goodness, "I would to God all the Lord's people could prophesy," so they take delight in seeing and hearing others' virtues, and thank God that others are better than themselves; as we may hear hereafter. But to manifest the truth of our observation before propounded, we have examples of other hypocrites, who were of the same disposition. First, in those counterfeit visitants of David, "In my adversity they rejoiced and gathered themselves together," (Psalm 35:15-16). So we read it; but the word in the original signifies, *in claudication mea, in my halting they rejoiced*; which is (Hebrews 12:13) applied to the soul sometimes, as well as to the body. This may signify as well the evil of sin, as that of punishment. David being put on hard adventures by Saul's persecution, sometimes was subject to halting, that is, to failings, and the discovery of many infirmities. These, when some heard or saw, they gathered themselves together and rejoiced at it, made themselves merry with it, though they would seem to him to be very sorry; and coming to visit him, would tear their clothes, and express much grief; as Tremellius understands the words. But now, who were the men that did this? The next verse tells you that, "Hypocritical mockers at feasts," that is, men indeed that dissembled much religion, but were but stark hypocrites, the good fellows of those times, that had many jovial and merry meetings; and when they were assembled together, they dealt with David, as the Philistines did in a like case with Sampson (sent for him to make them sport) made him, and his infirmities, his halting, their table-talk; mocking, and making jests upon him. "Hypocritical mockers at feasts." And this David, having former experience of, he fears and prays against in another place. "I said, Hear me, lest my enemies rejoice over me; when my foot slippeth, they magnify themselves against me. For I am ready to halting," (Psalm 38:16-17) that is, to show my infirmities, in my trials and afflictions. And upon this ground he enforces his supplication, for strength and grace; because his hypocritical enemies would vaunt, insult, and triumph in his failings. The prophet Jeremiah had similar experiences in his times; "They waited (he says) for my halting; peradventure he will be enticed, and we shall prevail against him," (Jeremiah 20:10). There were some that watched the prophet, to see if they could catch him in some untruth; and to this purpose, they laid baits to entice him, and snares to entrap him, that so they might have occasion to insult over him, that Jeremiah himself was taken napping, as well as others. And who were the men that thus watched him? "All my familiars (he says) the men of my peace;" hypocrites, that would come to inquire of him, what was the word of the Lord. "Report, say they, and we will report it." False prophets would come to him, pretending that they waited on him, and depended on him, as a true Prophet of God; but the truth was, they waited for his halting, so that they might triumph over him, that he was much overtaken as themselves; which argues, "That hypocrites, however seemingly good, yet secretly they take delight and contentment in others' infirmities, or sinfulness;" which being a naughty disposition, and a devilish, you may wonder it should be incident to any reasonable living man. We will therefore see its grounds.

Reason 1. Comfort in company. First, a corrupt heart finds comfort in company. It is true of sin, as well as of misery, *Solamen miseris socios habnisse.* It is not so with good hearts; they do not care how many companions they have in good, how few in evil, either of sin or punishment. "Let thy hand, I pray thee, be against me, and against my father's house. as for these sheep, what have they done?" Contrarily, the harlot having her own child dead, would be contented to have here neighbor's to be dead too; this would be a kind of comfort and contentment to her. Just so is it in sin with naughty hearts; they comfort themselves in others' sinfulness; and they have it from their father the devil. So soon as he had sinned, and was hurled down to hell, his next work was to entice man, and make him sinful, so to make him also miserable. But what comfort can a man take in wicked company?

1. It will make a foil for his seeming goodness; others' badness, opposed against his goodness, makes him seem better, as his goodness makes others to seem worse, as black and white are opposed, making each other appear more eminent in their kind. A sun's burnt face is white, compared with a black moore. The Pharisee was a saint to the publican. And this was the very intent of the Pharisee, to bring in these examples of the grossest sinners, to make himself seem more gloriously virtuous. Abraham's faith was sublimated and exalted by the infidelity of those times. The chastity of Lot was more orient, that, like a precious pearl, it lay in the dunghill of filthy Sodom. And their sin was aggravated, and, if I may so say, *magnified,* by the

opposition of Lot's chastity. A hypocrite, such as this Pharisee was, is a vainglorious creature, seeking by all means to magnify himself; and therefore glad to fetch luster to his seeming virtues from others' vices. Yes, *Genus virtutis est, esse minus vitiosus*, says one; *It is held a kind of virtue and honor in bad times, to be less vicious.* And with simple judgments, he passes for a just man that is no extortionist or oppressor; he seems to be very chaste, that is not a gross adulterer. The hypocrite knows this; and therefore if he can produce examples of affirmative or positive illness, supposes he shall find the honor, at least of a privative or negative goodness.

2. If he cannot attain this, to get a color to varnish his seeming goodness, yet to find a cover for his own badness will be a comfort. He is not now without an excuse to extenuate at least his own known badness. I am a sinner indeed, but not so bad as such and such; not as other men are, extortionists, adulterers, *etc.* men of good note and better parts, have done worse than I ever did. I am no extortionist, I thank God; I am no adulterer. And this is the common pleas of ignorant people, *I thank God, I am neither whore nor thief, as such and such are*; and so please themselves, and

comfort themselves, that they are not so bad as others are, and this is the use they make of others' badness.

3. This gives them hope of a good condition, notwithstanding their wicked lives. They hope they may be saved as well, yes before others that are worse than they in some particulars, especially if they are men that have had the reputation of godliness. David committed adultery and murder, Noah was drunk, so was Lot, and incestuous; many professors now are worse overseen than they are, they thank God. Yet these men were (at least hoped to be) saved; they lived and died God's children; and why may they not do with lesser sins? This is the common delusion of ignorant men. If they are not saved that are not extortionists, not adulterers, etc. what will become of those that are? They hope to escape as well as others.

4. This will serve to allay the discredit and shame of their own wicked courses; singularity in sin makes men more remarkable, and so more infamous. Community either makes it esteemed as no fault, or no crime, *Incipit esse licitum, quod incipit esse publicum*, that begins to be accounted lawful, which means to be public. And that ceases to be shameful, that most or many do. For this cause a sinner desires to infect

others, if he can, or at least is glad to find them infected, to qualify his own shame.

5. Lastly, if he can take comfort in none of these, yet in this he will, that he shall not be miserable alone. This we hear desperately out of the mouths of wicked men, if they do go to hell, they shall not go alone; there is good company in store there. Miserable comforters are they all; yet such comfort, the corrupt hearts of men (as the devil himself also does), sucks out of the falls and sins of other men. And this is the first reason of their joy in evil.

Reason 2. Envy. Another reason is that secret envy, which is the attendant of hypocritical pride. "Do you think the Scripture says in vain, the spirit that is in us lusteth after envy?" (James 4:5) Saint James says. There is in every proud heart a portion of envy, the nature of it is, as to grieve at others' good, so to rejoice at others' bad; whether of sin, or misery. "The ungodly shall see it," (Psalm 112:10) that is, the prosperity of the godly, "and it shall grieve him." Now this is certain, he that grieves at another's good will rejoice at his hurt or evil. And this is as true in moral good or evil, he that envies and consequently grieves at another's virtues or goodness (as every hypocrite does, he would have no thoughts as virtuous but himself) will certainly be glad, and please himself greatly with others' badness. This is true because (as we said) this adds a luster to his seeming virtues. A proud man cannot endure a competitor in goodness. The Pharisees did all they could to engross the name and honor of knowledge and religion to themselves; and therefore, when our blessed Savior was deservedly raised and magnified by the people above them, his honor was the object of their envy, and the matter of their torment and vexation. And when they had procured him to be put to death, how did they rejoice and insult upon him! The same may be seen of Joseph's brothers, (Genesis 37).

Reason 3. Hatred of goodness. A third and last reason is, from a secret hatred of goodness, however he may seem to love and favor it. A hypocrite, whatever shows he makes, yet does not *love* goodness; not in himself, much less in others. Indeed, it is the appearance he loves, because it brings him credit in the world; but he, "receives not the truth in the love of it," (2 Thessalonians 2:10). Yes, secretly he hates it, and hates to be reformed, as the Psalmist speaks; and it is no wonder, for he hates God, though perhaps he does not perceive it. Now this is a rule, as love and hatred are contrary affections, so they have contrary objects. Love good, and hate evil; or love evil, and hate good. Again, as those that love good in themselves or others cannot but joy and delight in beholding it; so those that hate good cannot but rejoice in the evil of others. A good man is pleased as well with others' good, as his own. An evil man is no less with others' illness, than his own. "Love (the Apostle says) rejoices not in iniquity, but rejoiceth in the truth," (1 Corinthians 13:6) or *with* the truth. "Love (he says) envieth not, it swelleth not, it vaunteth not itself (over others' infirmities) it behaveth not itself unseemly," (1 Corinthians 13:4). But hatred envies, swells, or is puffed up, vaunts itself, and behaves itself unseemly; and thereupon rejoices in iniquity. These are the grounds of the point.

Reason 4. The application. And now we come to make some application of this doctrine to ourselves; and we will (for better method and memory) reduce all we have to say to two heads. 1. The discovery of many for hypocrites, by the wrong uses they make of others' infirmities, or sinfulness. 2. The directions to the right uses that we should make.

The first use of this is, to use it as a light to discover a world of hypocrites, who by several ways manifest this naughty and cursed disposition, to rejoice or take delight in others' badness; and they are of many sorts. We will note some:

1. First, such as from the sight and knowledge of others' sins, take occasion to harden themselves in their sinful courses, and to strengthen themselves in their wickedness; comforting themselves in the company of others, and perhaps those of the better sort, as they are reputed; and so, "settle themselves upon their dregs," as Zephany speaks. Why (they say) many of the best of God's children have been subject to their faults and infirmities; done as bad, or worse perhaps than we, and yet were saved. Noah, David, Lot, and others in our own knowledge. But to discourage this conclusion, we propound to such a threefold consideration.

1] The difference between them and their copy. For, 1. they sinned of infirmity, these men of deliberation. They did not look at the examples of others that fell before them, to fall after them, which these men do. They purposed, resolved, swore they would keep God's commandments; so these never did. Therefore theirs were sins of infirmity, these of presumption. 2. They sinned, but they repented, and proportionably to their sin; David watered his couch with his tears; Peter wept bitterly; did not, as these men do, comfort themselves, and put off sorrow, with examples of others' fallings. And 3, they sinned, but not after repentance; Noah drunk but once and these never repent; or if they seem to do so, it was but in hypocrisy, as the continuance in their sin, by others' examples, demonstrates.

2] The issue and success of those sinners, whom they presume to follow. They sinned, but they hurt soundly; none so sharply out of hell. David had not only the sword threatened without, but had his bones broken within, (Psalm 51). If they knew how dear they paid for their sins, they would be loath to buy the pleasure at so dear a rate; therefore do not content yourselves with this poor comfort of their examples.

3] This would also be considered by such men, that this is a most fearful perverting of the Scripture, and the providence of God, in suffering others to fall before our eyes, to their own destruction, as the Apostle says some men do; and among all the uses that God intends therein, this is the worst and most dangerous. For if we ask, *Why did God suffer his children here to fall unto foul and scandalous sins, and record them in the Scripture?* One of these three may be said. First, for admonition; "These things were written for our admonition, that we should not lust as they lusted, nor murmur as they murmured; let him therefore that thinks he stands, take heed lest he fall," (1 Corinthians 10:11). Secondly, for comfort, that those that fall by infirmity, or otherwise, might have a ground of hope to rise again; *Who should ever rise, if they had not fallen? How apt are men, through their own corruption, and the devil's temptations, to despair?* None of God's children ever fell so low, so foully, would he say. Yes, Paul was a persecutor, and was received into God's mercy, that God might in him show an example, as of human frailty, so of God's mercy. Or thirdly, God in his providence suffers these falls, in former and present times, to make stumbling blocks for some, whom he purposes to destroy, to keep them from coming into the way of godliness; and so from the end, to which it leads, eternal life. It is certain, many stumble at this stone and rock of offense, the fallings and failings of God's people; and are either set at a stand in the profession of religion, as the people stood still at Asahel's carcass; or else turn quite back again, as if that were not the way, which such men walk in; who fall many times more heinously, more scandalously than mere natural men. They will not in sad and serious manner profess, because some profess religion, and are not, "Woe be to them, by whom the offense cometh," but woe also to the world, because of offenses; woe to the giver, and woe to the taker of offense. The way of heaven is a narrow and a straight way, and besides, slippery; he is more than a man, that does not fall sometimes, having so many stumbling blocks laid in his way by the flesh, the world, and the devil. But there is no other way but that. Now is he not a mad man that would refuse to walk a slippery way, suppose over ice, seeing there is no other way, because he sees many slip before him? Yet he is worse, who seeing his neighbor down, will not step over him, but *purposely* stumble, and fall with him; and then plead his example, to excuse his own falling. In this way do many men comfort themselves in the falls of others; and these are the first sort.

2. Secondly, another sort of hypocrites are those that, from the sight or knowledge of others' sins, take occasion to vent their gall against religion, and the profession of itself; to lay all the fault upon that, and to insult over the whole number of them that profess it, "This is their religion, these are your professors, your holy ones, thus they do, such they are all. *Fie* upon this

faction,"[4] as they sometimes said of David, "Fie upon thee, fie upon thee, we have seen it with our eyes:" Or, as some said of Saint Paul, the ring leader of the Nazarenes, as one called him. "Away with him, away with him, it is not fit that he should live." But to cool this heat a little, *consider:*

1) What hard measure these men exact of their brethren, they do to themselves; they will not allow them common, and human infirmities. Their brethren must live like angels, themselves like devils; and yet be counted honest men.

2) What inequality, if not iniquity is this in judgment? What partiality in judging? They can allow men of their own confederacy, many gross, not infirmities, but crimes. Some drunkards, some whoremasters, and what not? Yet they hear, honest men, good neighbors, only they have their infirmities. But if a professor of more godliness slips, and catches a fall (as who lives, and does not sin) his infirmities are made crimes; and himself proclaimed a hypocrite. Had these men lived in David's time, and seen his grievous falls, he should have heard, "Hypocrite, and counterfeit;" and "This is your holy David," and so he did from some, no

---

[4] *Fie* is used to express disgust or outrage.

doubt, "The drunkards made songs of him," perhaps for those or the like infirmities.

3) But what uncharitableness is this, to condemn all for one? There was Shem in Noah's family, an Ishmael in Abraham's, an Absalom in David's, a Judas in Christ's; shall any be so rash to say, they were all such? A gross falsehood; all are not such. There are many (blessed be the grace of God) that shine as lights, in the midst of a crooked and perverse generation. Many, whom the devil himself (except but common infirmities) cannot accuse justly of any scandalous sin.

4) What hypocrisy is this, to lay the faults of professors on religion, yes, that religion which themselves profess, at least in show? For papists to censure in this way of our religion were something tolerable; but for Protestants in this way to fly in the face of their own religion, what heart can hear with patience? They know, religion allows or teaches no such thing. "The grace of God, that brings salvation," teaches us to deny, "ungodliness and worldly lusts." The commandment is holy, and just, and good; though in the best profession some have their infirmities, and some indeed are hypocrites. And the truth is, this man that in this way strikes at the head or heart of religion,

through the sides of some weak professors' discovers his own hypocrisy. For if he did not hate religion (in the power of it) he could not so insult and rejoice in the shame of that, which yet he would seem to honor.

3. Thirdly, another sort are those who take occasion from men's sins, to insult over them, to scorn and despise them, as here the Pharisee did; "God, I thank thee, I am not as other men are." It is strange to see how superciliously some (perhaps more civilly honest men) carry themselves towards those who are more scandalously sinful, whether presumptuously or by infirmity. How do they entertain high thoughts of themselves, and their own goodness, in comparison of those? How highly they overlook them? How big they speak? How scornful? How reproachful? Like this Pharisee here, "This Publican," and those others elsewhere; "This people that knows not the law, are cursed." Or those their predecessors of old, "Stand farther off, I am more holy than thou. I thank God, I am not as other men." To let out his swelling, impostumated pride, I would propound these few considerations:

1] This is no great matter to boast of; a hypocrite, a heathen, a reprobate may be no extortionist, not unjust, no adulterer. Many such have been among the gentiles, as civilly honest as they.

2] This is but a negative kind of goodness, that is not to be better, but less ill than others; which is indeed a positive kind of illness, though in a lower degree. But to be less ill is not to be good; unless to be ill means to be good. And if he may be accounted good, who is less ill, there are scarcely any bad on earth; none almost so bad, but he may find worse, if not here, yet in hell. Cain and Judas might prove to be good and honest men, for no doubt there were some worse than them. No, I dare to be bold to say, there are many better than this negative man in hell; there are some, who not only were not adulterers, extortioners, *etc.* but chaste and charitable, and have done many good works in appearance. And therefore this is but a poor matter to boast of; not so bad as others on earth, not so deep as others in hell.

3] This may come from *restraining*, not from sanctifying grace; and what is a man the better for that? A lion in a chain cannot rage and devour, as he would do. The devil himself, that roaring lion, is held in the chain of God's almighty providence, so that he cannot do the mischief which he would. Their nature is never the better for that. You are no extortionist, no adulterer; perhaps you would, but did not dare, but *could* not. Is this a thing to boast of?

4] But grant all this, yet who may they thank for it? not themselves, not their own better nature, or disposition; but God that has chained up their corruption, and let loose others to their own heart's lusts. If others are so and so, they are to be pitied, not scorned. If any man is not so, he ought to be the more thankful, not proud and scornful; *Who made him to differ? What does he have that he has not received? Why then does he boast, as if he had not received it?*

5] Yet see the hypocrisy of men discovered. *I thank God*, says one. *I am not an extortionist, not an adulterer.* What great matter is this? All men are not extortionists or adulterers. Some have another lust predominant; their vein lies another way. One man hates adultery, but loves drunkenness. Another hates prodigality, but loves covetousness. Say then, you proud Pharisee, I am no slanderer, or detractor from other men's credit; I am not proud, but that you cannot say that you are not like the publican indeed, for he, though a sinner, was humble; you are a sinner, *and proud*. Several men have several ways to spend and vent their lust; *all are damnable.* Do not boast then that you are no adulterer when you are a blasphemer, or covetous or proud, that is *palpable hypocrisy.*

4. A fourth sort of hypocrites are such as delight and are glad to see or hear, or perhaps to tell and blaze abroad the faults and falls of others. Some have itching eyes, desirous to see or know. Some have itching ears, tickled and contented to hear the worst reports, especially of professors; and itching tongues that please themselves in raking in the infirmities of other men. Tell-tales, that like peddlers go up and down from house to house, and open their packs at every door. Did you not hear what such a one has done? I am sorry to speak it, I pray tell nobody; when secretly he is glad, and desirous that all should know it. Such a fellow was that cursed Shem, who could not satisfy his wickedness to see, but must needs run and tell his brethren of his Father's nakedness; whereas his brothers took no delight to see it. Therefore they went backward, and threw their garments over it, to show how displeasingly they heard so vile a report of their father. Such a hypocrite was Doeg, who (forsooth) was *detentus coram Jehova*, detained before the Lord at Nob, (1 Samuel 22:18) whether with conscience of the Sabbath,

or some vow, it does not matter; yet in the next chapter, turns informer against David. "I saw the son of Jesse coming to Nob." This he did, either to flatter and humor and curry favor with Saul; or to vent his secret plan and malice against David, whose virtues were more eminent, and whose shame eclipsed his. But David brands him for a stark hypocrite for his labor, and for a lying fellow, though he spoke but the truth. "Why boastest thyself in mischief, O thou mighty man? Thy tongue deviseth mischiefs, like a sharp razor, working deceitfully. Thou lovest evil more than good (for all thy fair pretenses of devotion) and lying rather than to speak righteousness. Thou lovest all devouring words, O thou deceitful tongue," (Psalm 52:1-4). Why (might some man say) Doeg told nothing but the truth; why then is he in this way complained on? Why? Because he spoke the truth with an ill mind, in an ill manner, boasting and insulting over David's infirmity, as if he were glad of this advantage, to ingratiate himself with Saul, and to do David a mischief. Such Doegs, there are too many now, hypocritical mockers at feasts (as David calls them) trencher-flies, who fall on the sores of those that profess godliness; to please some, to whom they know such news will be welcome;

men notwithstanding that seem sometimes very pious and devout, holy with the holy. This secret delight, to hear or tell others' infirmities, discovers them for hypocrites; and these are the fourth sort.

5. Another sort are, such as envy at others' goodness, or credit arising there. "Some preach Christ out of envy," said the Apostle; and how glad were they to spy out the failings of those that preached in sincerity? Now this is certain, he that is envious at others' goodness, will rejoice, or be much pleased with his badness. Paul was of another disposition; "Notwithstanding, whether in pretense, or in truth, Christ is preached, and therein I do rejoice, and will rejoice," (Philippians 1:18). Good men desire all men were as good, yes better than themselves; this they pray for. "I would to God (says Moses) that all the Lord's people could prophesy." "I would to God (says Paul to Agrippa) not only thou, but even all that hear me this day, were altogether such as I am." To conclude, do you see a man that is proud, vainglorious, and consequently envious? Certainly, that man cannot but take delight in seeing and hearing others' badness. Envy feeds itself upon others' evil; it is as pleasant to him, as his meat and drink. But to allay this cursed disposition in them

all, I propound but these three things to their consideration:

1] This argues that they are destitute of all true Christian charity and love of their brethren; "Love envieth not, love rejoiceth not in iniquity," its own or others. That man that should see his very enemy fall, and break a leg or arm, but the neck of his soul, if I may so say, and make himself and others sport with it, has put off man, and put on devil. The devil indeed rejoices at the falls of men. As there is joy in heaven for one sinner that repents; so, no doubt, there is joy in hell for one penitent that relapses. I may allude to Saint James. "If you have bitter envying and strife in your hearts (which will certainly cause rejoicing at others' evil) glory not, and lie not against the truth," (James 3:14-15). This wisdom (or folly rather) does not descend from above, but is earthly, sensual, devilish.

2] As they have no love of their brethren, so nor any love of God (whatever they may pretend) that can rejoice in his dishonor. Nothing more dishonors God, than the scandalous *lives* of *professing* Christians; and can you rejoice in that which grieves and dishonors him? Can any good child sport himself in his father's disgrace? I will say to you, as Paul to Elymas the sorcerer, "Thou child of the devil, thou enemy of all righteousness," no matter what pretense or profession you make.

3] This is enough to discover such for hypocrites; whatever show of religion they make, they indeed hate it. God himself challenges such, "To the ungodly (God says) what hast thou to do to preach my law, and to take my covenant in thy mouth; whereas thou hatest to be reformed?" (Psalm 50). In this (he might say) *I hate to be reformed.* Mark what follows; "Thou satest (in the seat of scorners) and spakest against thy brother, and hast slandered thine own mother's son." You take delight to be speaking of your brother, things either true or false, it does not matter; and the conclusion of this is that you are a hypocrite. No sound members of the body can delight itself in the disease or dishonor of a fellow-member. "If one member suffers, all the members suffer with it; if one member be honored, all the members rejoice with it," (1 Corinthians 12:26). Let these things be considered; and so we proceed to the second use.

2. Directions. And that is for direction, how to stand affected at others' badness, and what uses we ought to make, if (at least) we will approve our hearts

either to God or men, or ourselves to be sincere. To insult and be glad at others' badness, that they are worse than we, is a sign of a naughty and hypocritical heart. What then is to be done in such a case? We cannot but see daily the outflyings of other men's corruptions, into many foul and scandalous sins; and what use worldly men and hypocrites make of it, to triumph in their falls, we have heard already; which being considered, let us see what use we ought to make. We will reduce all to these four heads: 1. To humble us, 2. To make us thankful, 3. To make us pitiful and mournful, 4. To make us watchful.

1] Humility. The first use we should make is to humble us, in consideration of our common frailty. It was a heathen man's advice, "When thou beholdest other men's infirmities, reflect upon thine own heart, and ask thyself, *Numnam ego talis*? Did I never commit the same, or the like as bad?" Yes, the Apostle infers all meekness to be used to all men, upon this very ground. "For we ourselves were sometimes foolish, disobedient, serving diverse lusts," (Titus 3:3). Or, if not so, yet ask once more, may I not be so? May I not fall as foul as he? Have I not the same nature? The same corruption? Even this consideration the Apostle also urges; "If any man be overtaken with a slip or infirmity, you that are spiritual, restore him with the spirit of meekness, considering thyself, lest thou also be tempted," (Galatians 6:1). That sin (as well as misery) may befall every man, which befalls any man. Yes, we should be so far from insulting and rejoicing at it, that we should tremble at their fall, and at the justice of God in suffering it. To be given over to a man's own heart's lusts, is one of the most fearful judgments that can befall a man. "So I gave them up to their own heart's lusts, and let them follow their own imaginations," (Psalm 81:12); as if he did not know how to punish them worse. To punish a man with sinning, is the worst part to be trembled at, much more the greatest, If we see a man suddenly struck dead by the pestilence, or other disease, we are amazed, and tremble at it, (Acts 5:11); how much more ought we to do so, when we see a man struck down with sin? And that the rather, when we consider that it might have been our case, having the same nature, the same desert in both? We have as great sins to provoke God, to let our corruptions loose, to shame both ourselves and our profession. "Behold the goodness and severity of God," (Romans 11:22), as the Apostle in a like case. Goodness to you, severity to those that fall; mercy to you, justice to those; and when you behold, be humble and tremble. Tremble, I say, at his severity to them, and his goodness to you, if you continue in his goodness; otherwise (mark what follows) "...even thou also shalt be cut off," *shall be let loose*, and fall as foul as they are. "Thou wilt say then (to allude to the Apostle) They are fallen, but I stand upright," (verse 19). Well, they are fallen by unbelief, unthankfulness, or some other sin, by the justice and just judgment of God, "and thou standest by faith (*if* you have faith) be not high-minded, but fear." If God did not spare them, take heed lest he does not spare you. And that is the first use to be made of others' falls.

2] Thankfulness. A second is for thankfulness, that we are not so bad. The Pharisee supposed right, had he but proceeded right; had the manner been suitable to the matter, no man could have spoken better. It is worth an abundance of thanks that we are not as other men are, as has been largely proved in the former point. We will but borrow the remembrance of the chief heads, to quicken the exhortations, and then proceed to another. There is great reason we should say (with a more humble heart than the Pharisee) "God, I thank thee, that I am not as other men are, not an extortioner, *etc.*" I do not know what is the greater mercy, to forgive a sin when it is committed, or to prevent a sin from being committed. I will not dispute the case; but propound the reasons for our thankfulness.

1) If we consider the spawn and seed of corruption, which lies bedded in our hearts, waiting for opportunity to break out into the same enormities; there is not the vilest sin that ever was committed, that we would not potentially commit, if God did not *mercifully* restrain us. We admire and wonder at others' badness; we do not need, if we consider the root from where it proceeds, but rather wonder how we are not as bad, and admire God's goodness that we are not. It is, we said even now, one of the greatest judgments of God, to let corruption loose upon a man, and to deliver him into the power thereof. It is consequently one of the greatest mercies to have it chained up from breaking out. And therefore say humbly, "God, I thank thee, *etc.*"

2) In regard of the issues and consequences of sin committed, which are manifold and grievous miseries, which our eyes have seen overtake men for

their sins which they have committed. A wounded spirit, broken bones, as David calls them; sorrow, sickness, poverty, ignominy, shame to themselves, friends profession, and religion itself; death temporal, yes, and perhaps eternal, from all which are freed, by being kept from their sins. Consider what they would give to be innocent again, if possible; and think what a mercy it is, to be kept from their sin, and their misery. And then go and bless God, and say, "God, I thank thee," we cannot but stand amazed that many, and they in our opinion and their own, godly, learned, wise, have fallen into so many great and foul sins, to their own shame, sorrow, misery, and the scandal of religion. Why have we not fallen into the same pit? Are we better than them? Not at all. It is the *grace of God* that makes this difference between us. Blessed be God, and his grace for his mercy. O! then, do not insult over men wounded and fallen at our feet, do not rejoice at them, but with all humble thankfulness, adore and bless that grace that has preserved us from falling.

3] But it is not enough not to rejoice or triumph at the falls of others; it is also a duty required to mourn with them, and for them. This, I am sure, was the practice of holy men heretofore; so did David, "I was grieved to see the transgressors. Mine eyes gushed out with rivers of tears, because men keep not thy law," (Psalm 119:136). So did Saint Paul, in a case of scandalous sin, by the incestuous person. "Out of much affliction and anguish of heart, I wrote unto you with many tears," (2 Corinthians 2:4). "Some walk (he says) of whom I have told you before, and now tell you weeping," (Philippians 3). And there is very good reason for it. for,

a. Otherwise you are likely to fall into the same, or another sin that is as bad, and as scandalous. Into the same, first, for nothing better to preserve a man from the infection of other men's sins, then to be grieved and mourn for them. This kept just Lot from the hurt of Sodom's sins, living among them, that, "he vexed his righteous soul, in beholding their unclean conversation," (2 Peter 2). On this ground the Apostle told his Corinthians, that a, "little leaven would leaven the whole lump;" even infect them, that had not sorrowed for the sin committed by the incestuous person. Or if you escape the same, it is just with God to let you fall into another sin as bad and infamous; because you show no compassion and mourn for other's sins, much more, if you in the least manner rejoice at his fall. The unmercifulness and scorn of men is sometimes thus requited. What Solomon says of an enemy, may very well be applied to this purpose. "Rejoice not at thine enemy when he falleth (into misery, or sin) neither let thine heart be glad, when he stumbleth; lest the Lord see it, and it displease him, and he turn his hand from him, upon thee," (Proverbs 24:17); and suffer you to fall into the like, or as bad a sin, to find as little mercy and compassion, or as much scorn and contempt as you have shown your brother. I do not doubt that this has overtaken many of God's children; they have been let go, to fall, because they have not pitied and mourned with others that have fallen by them. God cannot endure that men, subject to the like infirmities, should be proud and insult, or be merciless and pitiless towards others; and therefore oftentimes pays them in their own coin.

b. But if not so, yet you shall be guilty of other sins, for which you have not mourned; much more, if rejoiced at it. The Apostle charges his Corinthians for a double fault in this kind. One, that they did not mourn for that scandalous sin; another, that they were puffed up, swelled against him, insulted over him. And this made them doubly guilty of his sin. Contrarily, when they had mourned for that sin, he gives them their acquittance, "Behold this very thing, that ye have been godly sorry," (2 Corinthians 7:11) what apology it has worked out for you. You have shown yourselves free in this matter. It may seem a paradox, but is a truth. A man is guilty of all those sins of the times he does not mourn for. But if he shall add, to rejoice at them, or take pleasure in those that do them, as the Pharisee did, he shall be doubly, yes, triply guilty of them.

c. And if guilty of the sin, liable to the punishment. "Be not partakers of her sin, lest ye be partakers of her judgment," is a caution prescribed especially in the case of Babylon; but may extend to any nation, or particular person's sin. This was once proved on the contrary, in a common destruction, the mourners were only preserved. "Go (he says) and set a mark upon the foreheads of all those that mourn for the abominations committed in the city," (Ezekiel 9:4); and then smite the rest, and spare none. Let this be considered.

d. The last use we are to make upon the view and consideration of other's falls and infirmities is to be more watchful over our own hearts and ways. The Apostle makes the conclusion for us. "Let him therefore that thinks he stands, take heed lest he fall," (1 Corinthians 10:11). Not only their punishments, but their sins are written for our example, that we do not sin as they did. They are written for our admonition; they murmured, they committed idolatry, they fell into fornication, they were tempted; we are made of the same mettle, subject to the same infirmities. Let no man therefore insult over their falls, on conceit of his own strength; but let him that thinks he stands, take heed lest he fall. The same may be said concerning those who fall into scandalous sins in our own knowledge. "Consider thyself, lest thou also be tempted." This exhortation is very seasonable, to walk circumspectly, to walk exactly, especially to those who make a more than ordinary profession of religion, considering:

a] Our own frailty, even the strongest of us; we are made of the same matter, have the seed of the same sins in us. But when we see men far better than ourselves so foully overtaken, how should we choose but tremble, and watch and pray against our own weaknesses? That place of Nehemiah is pertinent, "Did not Solomon King of Israel sin by these things? Yet among many nations, there was no King like unto him, who was beloved of God. Nevertheless him did outlandish women cause to sin," (Nehemiah 13:26). Therefore, the argument is strongly enforced. Did Solomon? Did David? Did Peter so stumble, and fall so foully and heinously? Men of admirable strength, wisdom, and piety? Who then may not fear to fall? If the cedars of Lebanon were so shaken, so broken, how had the lesser underwood need to look to their standing? If men of years and strength slip and fall, how had children need to look to themselves?

b] Considering the issues ordinarily of the falls of those that profess godliness, the sinful example of a wicked man hurts much, but nothing to that of a Professor. For:

(1) This more hardens some that are wicked in their courses. Why the best men have their infirmities. No, they do sometimes as bad as we; Noah was drunken, David adulterous, *etc.* and yet good men, and saved.

(2) This more grieves those that are good. Nothing wounds their souls more, than to see their fellow brethren fall so foully; Paul was grieved much for his countrymen the Jews that were not, nor would be converted; but more, I believe, for that sin and scandal of the incestuous person, who was a Christian.

(3) This more disgraces religion, and consequently keeps men off from being religious. The very rumor and slander of the primitive Christians, that they were incestuous and adulterous, was a strong engine of the devil to keep many from being converted, especially the more civil sort of heathens. They could not love that religion that allowed (as they were told and believed) such monstrous iniquities. And at this day, what keeps the Turks and Jews from being Christians, but the wicked lives of many professing Christianity? Among us Christians, what withholds many papists from converting, but the dissolute lives of many Protestants? Among us Protestants, what keeps many, otherwise civilly honest, from being altogether Christians, that is, truly godly, but the scandalous lives of some professors? That Indian, labored by the Jesuits to become a Christian, having asked, what became of the Spaniards when they die, and of his own forefathers; and being answered that the latter went to hell, the former to heaven; replied that he would rather go to hell with his forefathers, than to heaven with the Spaniards. "It cannot be (our Savior says) but offenses will come; but woe to the man by whom they come:" Woe to the world, because of offenses; woe to the

takers; woe, yes, twice woe to the givers. It would be better for a millstone to be hung about their necks, and they cast into the sea, than that they should lay such stumbling blocks in the way of others; O therefore be watchful, be circumspect, walk wisely towards those that are outside; Give no offense to the Jew nor Gentile, nor to the Church of God.

(4) Lastly, this more dishonors not only religion, but God himself; when the doctrine suffers, the name of God suffers with it. It opens the mouths of wicked men, even against God himself. You may judge of Christ, by the lives of those that are called Christians, said Salvian of old. If Christ their Master were good, and his doctrine good, these Christians could not be so bad. Therefore the Apostle seriously advises people to be exact in their religion, "lest the word of God be blasphemed," (Titus 2:5), as a teacher or allower of such things as are dishonest. And again, "that the Name of God, and his doctrine be not blasphemed," (1 Timothy 6:1). And to whom does he speak this? First, to wives, and they of the ordinary sort too. He would have them be lovers of their husbands, lovers of their children, sober, chaste, keepers at home, obedient to their own husbands, that the, "Word of

God be not blasphemed," (Titus 2:5). Then to servants, "Let as many servants as are under the yoke, count their own masters worthy of all honor, that the Name and doctrine of God be not blasphemed," (1 Timothy 6:1). Alas (some might say) what credit or discredit can a poor woman, or a poor servant do to religion? Yes, much either way. Therefore the Apostle Peter speaks of wives, that he would have them virtuous and pious, "that their husbands which believe not, might be won by the conversation of the wives," (1 Peter 3:1-2). And the Apostle Paul speaks of servants, that "they should be obedient to their own masters in all things, careful to please, not answering again, not purloiners; but showing all good faithfulness," (Titus 2:9). To what end and purpose? "That they may adorn the doctrine of God our Savior in all things." The poorest and meanest professor that is, may do much good or much hurt to religion; and therefore my exhortation and adjuration to you all that profess religion more than ordinarily, whether you are high or low, rich or poor, masters or servants, is that you walk circumspectly, exactly, watchfully over your hearts and ways; and that the rather, because there are many observers, (Psalm 27:1), as David calls his enemies, that watch for your halting, and will rejoice to see even the meanest professor slip or fall; and be ready to insult over not only you, but your religion, your fellow-brethren, yea in a manner, your God. I would have you therefore to abstain, not only from gross evils, but even, "from the very appearance of evil," (1 Thessalonians 5:22). Not only to be just and faithful, and sober and chaste, and true in all your words, promises, dealings, but to carry yourselves so fairly, so openly, so clearly honest, and godly, that those that watch for occasions, may not have so much as the least ground to fasten a suspicion on; but may be ashamed, and (if God please) be converted, or convinced, when they shall behold your blameless conversation. Do but thus walk, and you shall honor God, honor your fellow-brethren, (be you never so mean) honor religion; and religion and God himself shall honor you here, and in the end crown you with glory and immortality. Amen.

THE LAWFULNESS OF DOING GOOD OUT OF HOPE OF REWARD

Against the New Family of Love, the Antinomians.

"Which hope we have as an anchor of the soul, sure and steadfast, and entering into that which is within the veil," (Hebrews 6:19).

"That we may receive a full reward," (2 John 1:8)

The Apostle having propounded an admonition, to circumspection, in the former part of this verse, (Look to yourselves) enforces it by a double danger, of a double loss; Loss of labor, (that we lose not the things which we have wrought,) and loss of reward; (but that we may receive a full reward.) These words then, are the second ground of enforcement, taken from the fear or danger of a second loss; and there are in it considerable, these three *particulars*:

1. The thing expected, *A reward.*
2. The degree of that reward, *A full reward.*

3. The expectation of that full reward; *that we may receive it*; Look to yourselves, that we may receive it.

Explanation. Of the two former, we have already spoken in past teachings; we are now to dispatch the last. And the words carry this meaning with them; As if the Apostle should have said, "We (or you, for the copies differ) do expect to receive a full reward, yes a full reward of our labor (and you of yours;) if you do not circumspectly look to yourselves, we, or you, or both, shall come short of your hope; and lose, if not all, yet at least, some part of our reward; our reward shall not be so full as we expect." Therefore I admonish and exhort you to look to yourselves, lest we and you, losing the things which we (or you) have worked, also lose our reward. Look to yourselves that our expectation may not be frustrated but that we may indeed receive what we earnestly expect.

The conclusion here resulting will be this. That it is lawful (if not necessary) for the best men, for their better encouragement in the service of God, to have an eye upon the promised reward. Or thus, hope of reward is not altogether unlawful, in doing of our duty to God. This point, were it not for the ignorant clamors and presumptuous importunity of some, need not any great confirmation, the thing is so apparent, both in Scripture and reason. But that we may give satisfaction to those that doubt, or conviction to those that deny this truth; we will bestow some pains in making it good. And *that*:

1. By those gracious promises of God made to us in the Scripture; which, what else can they import, but a liberty and lawfulness at least, to make use of them, to the best advancement of our performances? We instance in some. That to Abraham, is of this kind, to this purpose, "Fear not, Abraham;" Why? "I am thy Shield, and thy exceeding great reward," (Genesis 15:1). And another, "I am God almighty, walk before me, and be upright," (Genesis 17:1). As if he should say, "Go on Abraham, in thy obedience to my commands, fear nothing; and for thy encouragement take this my gracious promise, (which forget not to remember and make use of) I will be thy Shield to defend thee; and thy exceeding great reward, to recompense thee for all thy losses thou undergoes for my sake." Look often on this promise, and be encouraged to go on cheerfully. That is a most pregnant place, where Moses lays down a catalogue of blessings promised to obedience; "If thou shalt hearken diligently unto the voice of the Lord thy

God, Blessed shalt thou be in the city, and blessed in the field," (Deuteronomy 28:1, 3). To what purpose all this, if those people might not, in performance of their obedience, cast an eye upon them? Moses might have saved that labor both of repeating and writing, and barely have propounded the will of God, and so have left them to choose whether they would obey, or not. As Kings proclaim their pleasure, without any promise of reward, or particular penalty it is at the subjects' peril, if he refuses to yield to obedience. But lest any should say, this was indeed a course fit for the pedagogy of the law; Children must be drawn with sweet allurements, as those with a land flowing with milk and honey; but the Gospel gives more grace, and therefore, now, love must supply the place, both of hope and fear. We take some of this in the New Testament. Our blessed Savior himself, the only Lawgiver, not only implicitly, in propounding blessedness to those particular virtues; but explicitly and plainly, (Matthew 5:12). He provokes them to rejoice and be exceedingly glad, in persecution, upon this very argument of our text, "For great is your reward in heaven." So, "Love your enemies, and your reward shall be great," (Luke 6:35). In this way Saint

Paul says, "Seeing therefore we have these promises, (to be the sons and daughters of God), Let us, (on the sight of these promises, and certain expectation of their performance) cleanse ourselves from all filthiness of the flesh and spirit," (2 Corinthians 7:1). And Saint Peter treads in the same steps, "Wherefore, beloved, seeing ye look for such things (a new heaven, and a new earth, according to his promise) be diligent, that ye may be found without spot and blameless," (2 Peter 3:14). I could be infinite in such parallel places; which (I say again) are all needless arguments, if so we may not make use of them, by exercising of our hope, to excite our diligence in those enjoined duties.

2. By the commands of Scriptures, founded upon those promises, to exercise our hope; how often do we hear it in the Old Testament; "Hope in the Lord; Hope in his mercies," (Psalm 42:4, 130:7). Now what is hope, but the expectation of those things which God has promised? Can a man expect them, and not hope for them? Can a man hope for them, and not look at them? Can he look at them, hope for them, or expect them, and not be provoked to those duties to which they are promised? We have one pertinent place for all, and that in the New Testament; it is Saint Peter's. "Gird

up the loins of your mind (your fainting hearts) be sober, and hope to the end for the grace (*i.e.* the glory) that is to be brought unto you at the revelation of Jesus Christ," (1 Peter 1:13). Hope to the end, or perfectly for that grace; and let hope be the girdle to gird up the loins of your mind. We must hope; therefore we may hope for a reward.

3. By the many instances, even of men regenerate, that looked at the reward promised. It is a general description of good and holy men in Scriptures; by their hope, and expectation of the promises. "Old Simeon waited for the Consultation of Israel," (Luke 2:25). "Joseph of Arimathea looked for the kingdom of God," (Mark 15:43). "Abraham looked for a city," (Hebrews 11:10). "We look for the Savior, who shall change our vile bodies," (Philippians 3:20). "Looking for the blessed hope," (Titus 2:13), "Seeing ye look for such things," (2 Peter 3:14). No more; their hope is called, the earnest expectation of the creature, (Romans 8:19) the Greek word which signifies such an *intense expectation*, as men express, when they look for some longed for friend, and stand fixing their eyes, and thrusting them almost out of the holes of their heads; as if they would send their eyes to meet them, whom they think too

long in coming. Yes, if more may be, the Apostle has another word, more emphatic, "They saw the promises afar off (by their faith) and embraced them, saluted them (so is the word) by their hope," (Hebrews 11:13). They *looked so earnestly* for them, as if they had sent their hearts before to salute them, which yet they might not perfectly enjoy. In particular:

1] Moses, a man of God without exception, and regenerate (lest any might object; we do not deny the use of these to unregenerate men, to draw them on, until love may come in place). This Moses, (I say) as good as he was, was glad to strengthen himself from the hope of reward, "He had an eye (one eye at least) to the recompense of reward," (Hebrews 11:26). If Moses, who was so good a holy a man as Moses could be, and it seems, need of this help, how much more we, who (boast what we will) I fear come far short of Moses' perfection. If any shall say (as some will) this was under or before the law; but the time of the Gospel, is a time and state of greater perfection; Take another *example*:

2] Primitive Christians. Those Christians whom Saint Paul testifies of in this manner, "You suffered with joy the spoiling of your goods," (Hebrews 10:34).

What ground of encouragement did they have? Did they do it purely and merely out of the strength of their love? Hear the rest, "Knowing that you have in heaven a better and more enduring substance." A man will not throw away foul water, (we say) until he had hope at least, of fair water coming. Nor would they (I suppose) so joyfully have parted with their earthly substance, had they not had an expectation of a heavenly substance. But did they do well to make this use of their hope? Was it not a weakness in them, to be checked, rather than allowed? Mark what follows. He encourages them to it still; still to make use of their hope; "Cast not away therefore your confidence, which hath great recompense of reward," (Hebrews 10:35). But lest any should say, these were weaklings in the faith, and not perfect in love, I *add*:

3] Adam in innocence. who certainly, being created after the Image of God, was perfect in righteousness and holiness; and if ever man did, he might love the Lord, with all his might, yet even Adam (it seems) had need of some helps, that we now have, the fear of punishment on the one side, "In the day thou eatest, thou shalt die the death;" and hope of reward on the other side, "Do this, and thou shalt live," which was the tenure of the *old covenant*, as we all know. If Adam, much more we should know. If any yet shall say, Adam's was but a natural love, but ours now is supernatural; I add but one *more*:

4] Christ himself, the second Adam, both perfect and strong in every way, and therefore (we may think) did not need such help, as we do. Yet Christ himself used this support of his hope, and of reward set before him. The Apostle is plain, "Who, for the joy that was set before him, endured the cross and despised the shame," (Hebrews 12:2). Would we think Christ himself as strong as he was, would use this help, if it were not lawful to be used? Or shall we think ourselves stronger than he, that we can go without it? All which (to add no more) are a sufficient justification of the point propounded. But we have to confirm it.

4. By reasons why it is lawful, yes useful for us so to do.

1] Our weakness, which casts upon a necessity of all the helps that can be afforded us. It is true that Saint John speaks, "Perfect loves casts out all fear; and he that feareth is not perfect in love," (1 John 4:18). And it may peradventure be applied as well to hope; for I suppose, both Adam and Christ were perfect in love, and yet made use of their hope. And we shall hear later, that even in heaven, the saints both now have, and ever shall have use of their hope. But grant this for the present, "Perfect love casts out all hope," and needs no help but her own. Then I assume, but no man living is perfect in love; and therefore no man living can do without his hope, to be assistant to the imperfections of his love. "He that hopeth (I grant for the present too) is not perfect in love." But I assume again, we are not indeed perfect in love; and therefore we have need of hope. We know but in part, and therefore we believe but in part, and therefore hope but in part, and therefore love but in part; and therefore yield but a partial and imperfect obedience. Our obedience is measured by the degree of our love, our love by our hope, our hope by our faith, our faith by our knowledge; which being but in part, causes an imperfection in all the rest. The truth is (however some presume upon their strength) our weakness is such, that while we carry about with us the old man, we must expect to go stooping a little to the ground; and support ourselves with these two staves, of fear for the left hand, and hope for the right hand, to sure up our love from falling in the way.

2] Our humility requires as much; that seeing God himself (who knows us better than we know ourselves, and pities us as a father his children) allows us these helps. It is fit that we should with all thankfulness make our use of them. When God had said, "It is not good for man to be alone, I will make him an helper fit for him;" had Adam, out of the confidence of his own strength, as being innocent, and free from all sinful concupiscence, refused so gracious a tender, I suppose it would not have been well taken. The Lord himself, of his own good pleasure, proffered Ahaz a sign, "Ask thee a sign, ask it in the depth, or in the height above," (Isaiah 7:11). And he returns peremptorily, out of a foolish modesty, "I will not ask, neither will I tempt the Lord:" But mark how roundly the Prophet takes him up, "Hear ye now, O house of David, is it a small thing for you to weary men, but will you weary my God also?" It is not humility, but horrible pride and presumption to refuse and reject God's offers (on whatever pretenses of strength) and in a manner to scorn his helps, which he had never granted, but out of his infallible knowledge of our necessity. It is not good (God says) for love to be alone, I will allow her *hope* and (if need be) *fear* too, to be her helpers. It becomes then our modesty, in a humble sense and acknowledgement of our well known weakness, to accept and make use of our so graciously allowed *Helper*.

And so having sufficiently confirmed the point, that it is lawful, yes very useful for us to make use of our hope, in eyeing the promised reward; Let us make it yet more useful to ourselves, by application. It will yield us the *following*:

1. Confutation, of the conceited perfection of the new family of love, if I may so call them; who no less ignorantly than presumptuously cry down this doctrine, that I have so strongly confirmed. I refer to the *antinomians*, or, if you will, the *anomists* of our time; who pretend that they are so full of love, that they scorn to be beholden either to fear or hope. They do nothing, they, either for fear of punishment, or hope of reward; but all out of pure and mere love of God. Neither do they think a child of God, a regenerate man, ought to do anything with respect to either to the one or the other. For the fuller and clearer conviction of their error, we proceed in this method and manner, first by way of opposition of our former truth to their error. Secondly, by way of proposition of the many absurdities that will follow upon that opinion. Thirdly,

by way of exposition of the principal grounds of that their error.

1. Where they say, a regenerate man ought to do nothing out of hope of reward, but all out of love; which perhaps has received warmth and strength from that common received position of some divines, "That a child of God should serve God, though there were neither heaven to reward him, nor hell to punish him." I answer:

1] It is one thing to say what we should do; another what we do, or *can* do. The command indeed is, "Thou shalt love the Lord thy God will all thy heart," which if it were perfectly performed, might, perhaps, exclude the use of hope or fear; but let me see that man that ever did so love God that dared say, he *did* so; except the old catharists, and insolent papists, and these late upstart perfectionists. What? Are these men more perfect than Moses? Yet he had an eye to the recompense of reward. Are they better than Saint Peter? I do not doubt he loved Jesus Christ as well and as strongly as they; and presumed on the strength of that love, as much as they can do, that though all men denied him, yet he would not. And yet you know how shamelessly he denied his Master three times. But what? Are they stronger than Adam in innocence? His love, though supported both with hope and fear, failed him miserably, as lamentable experience tells us. However, though they do not hold to, some of them with little less than blasphemy to say, they are as perfect as Christ, and are they "Christed" along with Christ. Yet, I hope they have not yet come to that height of pride, to think themselves more perfect than Christ. Christ, who, for the joy that was set before him, endured the cross. What stranger presumption is this? I think I see them like little children, that have newly gotten their feet, who, proud and confident of their own strength, refuse the hand of the nurse; and will needs be going alone; until falls and broken faces teach them more wit. Certainly, this presumption of theirs, presages some fearful fall, to the disgrace of their profession, and scandal of religion; Let them but remember Saint Peter, and I will say no more, but with Saint Paul, "Let him that thinks he stands, take heed lest he fall," (1 Corinthians 10).

2] I add, their argument is infirmed and insufficient. A Christian must do *all* out of love, therefore nothing out of hope, or expectation of reward. This is to make the graces of God to fall out one with another, which sweetly agree; a good thing may be done in the love of God, and yet in hope of reward too. Hope and love are *not* contraries, but coordinate, like a pair of twin sisters, the daughters of one mother, Faith; or rather subordinate, and therefore may well concur to the producing of the same effect. We may say, (as the Apostle of faith says) *Hope works by love*, and love works from hope; as the soul works by the hand, and the hand works from the soul. And indeed, Love proceeds more immediately from hope than from faith. These three, (this is their order) "Faith, Hope, Love." Faith is the ground of things hoped for, and so of hope; and hope is the ground of love, as love of obedience. Why then should love thrust out hope, her mother, from any influence into her actions? It is in love, but yet by hope.

3] I say yet further, (*ex abundant*) whether we ever shall be so perfect, as to do all our services to God out of pure love, and nothing at all out of hope whether here on earth, or hereafter in heaven, is a disputable question. It seems probable that we shall not; I give my reasons, but submit them to the censure of the judicious. They are *these*:

1) Our love of God depends on our *knowledge* of God, (*ignoti nulla cupido*). Our knowledge of God is only

of his back parts, as himself calls them; which are such qualities, as have respect to us, "The Lord is merciful, gracious, longsuffering," (Exodus 34:6), not such as describe him absolutely in himself, as he is goodness itself. His goodness is absolutely only known to himself, and therefore only (so) loved by himself. I conclude then, we cannot love but with respect to his goodness to us, which is the object of our faith and hope; and so not without some mixture of hope; that's the first.

2) Self-love used rightly, (if moderate) is a natural impression of God on a man's soul; and therefore (it seems) to make a man love anything for itself, without some respect to himself, would be to destroy man's nature; "Praise the Lord, for he is good." Why? "For his mercy endureth forever."

3) Love proceeds from hope, as the effect from the cause. For therefore we love a thing, because we hope to receive some good from that thing; we do not (properly and directly) hope in anything because we love it, but only by accident, in as much as we believe, we are beloved of it. Therefore, it will follow, that we cannot love God, but because we first hope in him, as

the Author of all our good; and so hope will ever have and added ingredient to our love.

4) This is certain, in the judgment of the best divines, that the saints in heaven now have not lost their hope; they live in hope of the resurrection of their bodies, "My flesh shall rest in hope," (Psalm 16:9). No, nor after the resurrection ever shall lose their hope; though there be some difference between our hope now, and then theirs and ours. For ours, 1. Arises from faith, theirs from sight, 2. Ours is with labor and contention, theirs without all difficulty, 3. Ours is imperfect, theirs perfect. That received opinion of divines, that faith and hope shall cease in heaven; is not to be understood of the essence, or substance of those graces; but of their imperfection, and manner of their use. Faith shall be perfected by vision, and hope by fruition. We shall then see what we now believe; and enjoy, what we now hope for. Yet there shall still be use of both faith and hope; in as much as there shall forever be something that we shall never fully see; something that we shall never totally and together enjoy. The infinite essence and goodness of God, which no creature can comprehend, and the eternity of happiness, which no creature can at once and together

possess; and therefore shall have use of faith to believe the one, and hope to expect the other. Those exceptions, therefore of the schoolmen, may be easily answered both concerning faith and hope, "That because faith is that by which we believe what we do not see; and in heaven shall see that which now we believe, therefore it is impossible that faith should remain." And again, because we hope for that which we do not have; and in heaven, have in possession, that we now hope for, therefore it is impossible that hope should remain in heaven; For I assume, against himself; but in heaven, there shall be always something which we shall not see; and something we shall not enjoy, (without any derogation to our happiness) unless he will deify the creature. Therefore, there shall be still use of faith and hope in heaven. And this may be illustrated by the contrary fear of the damned; which fear being (contrary to hope) an expectation of evil to come, though the fear that wicked men now have of hell shall cease, when they once come in hell, fear being turned to present sense and feeling; yet they shall be tormented with the fear and expectation of the eternal *succession* of their torments, which shall be one of the worst parts of their hell. So on the contrary side; though hope in the godly, in regard of the complement of their happiness, shall cease, being turned into fruition; yet in regard of the eternity of that fruition, their hope shall be extended to eternity. And this shall be no small portion of their happiness. His distinction between the fear of the damned, and hope of the blessed; that fear may better be in the damned, than hope in the blessed, because (*forsooth*) in the one there shall be a succession of punishments, and so there shall be a respect of fruition or time to come; and in the other, the glory shall be without succession, after a certain participation of eternity, in which there is neither time past, nor to come, but only present. I say, this distinction is not true, (as I suppose) because there is the same succession of happiness in heaven, as of torments in hell; in regard of the creatures, who being finite, cannot infinitely at once enjoy their eternal happiness. God only, being infinite and only eternally at once and together enjoying his own happiness. But enough of that. I now rejoin my main point, if there is, (as is probable) a continued existence of hope, and we shall have always hope attending upon our love, it is as probable that hope shall not be idle, but exercised often, if not continually, in viewing of its object, and that view cannot but excite our love to all holy obedience, and that *forever*. If now, then *hear:*

2. The many absurdities that will follow, if that opinion may be granted, that a Christian has no use of his hope to encourage himself in the service of God.

1] They vilify, yes nullify the promises of God, made to what us in Scripture, at least in regard of a regenerate man. For to what end are the promises made to our obedience, if, for the better and more cheerful performance of our obedience, we may not, by the eye of hope, look at them? To what purpose were colors made, if the eye must be debarred the sight of them? Or musical sounds, if the ear may not be permitted to hear them? Take away the use of the sense, and take away the object of that sense. Take away hope and away with all the promises.

2] They cannot evacuate hope; but all other graces will vanish with it. The graces of God are like a chain, draw but one link, all the rest will follow; "Add to your faith virtue." Take away hope, and take away all.

1) Joy; which (much of it) arises from hope. "Rejoicing in hope," (Romans 12:12). "We rejoice in hope of the glory of God," (Romans 5:2). "Lively hope-

wherein ye rejoice," (1 Peter 3:6). Yes the greatest and strongest part of our joy springs from hope; "That we might have strong consolation, who, for a refuge, have laid hold on the hope set before us," (Hebrews 6:18).

2) Patience; which likewise is the daughter of hope, "If we hope for the things we see not, we do with patience wait for them," (Romans 8:25) called therefore the, "patience of hope," (1 Thessalonians 1:3). "For the joy set before him, endured the cross," (Hebrews 12:2).

3) Faith itself is likewise in danger; for though faith is the mother of hope, yet hope is the staff and strength of faith; and were it not for hope, faith itself would soon languish; *Sanguis fide, spes.* Hope is as the blood of faith. In the body, the blood is *vehiculum anima*; the chariot of the soul, the life running in the blood; take away the blood, and you take away life. So take away hope, and faith will soon expire; and therefore it is that faith and hope are so often joined together in Scripture; "That your faith and hope might be in God," (1 Peter 1:21). "We, through the spirit, wait for the hope of righteousness, by faith," (Galatians 5:5). And we are said to be "saved by hope," (Romans 8:24) as well as by faith. Take away hope, and take away faith.

4) Love also will not be long after, if you take away hope; for love itself (as I said) proceeds from hope, as well, and more immediately than from faith. This is their order, in regard of causality and generation, as the schoolman calls it; "Faith, Hope, and Love." Faith produces hope, and hope produces love, because hope to obtain those good things promised to, and believed by faith. Therefore we are moved to love him, that has promised, and will perform them. "Faith says (devout Bernard says) there are great and glorious things laid up for God's saints. Hope says, they are reserved for me. Love says, I run to them and embrace them. Faith believes them, hope expects them, and love at last enjoys them." And this is true, "Look how much a man believes, so much he hopes; how much he hopes, so much the more he loves." Love indeed proceeds from faith and hope, as the Holy Spirit proceeds from both the other persons of the Trinity. Take away hope then, and you destroy not only this Trinity, these three, faith, hope, and charity; but also the unity of procession, and the very essence of love; as the joint issue of hope and faith. In a word, hope both breeds and perfects love; we could not so love God for what he has done, but for the hope of what he will do; so that I may apply that of the

Apostle here, "If we have hope only in this life, we were of all men most miserable," (1 Corinthians 15:19). Those then that stand so much for love, to the vilifying, yes nullifying of hope, will in the end prove in themselves a nullity of love. Little hope, little love. No hope, no love at all.

5) Lastly, (which they think little about) all Christian obedience is in this way endangered, or at least, a great part of it. For take away hope, even hope of reward, and what will become of all good works? Does every reasonable creature not work out of hope? "He that ploweth, ploweth in hope; and he that thresheth, thresheth in hope," (1 Corinthians 9:10). The soldier wars in hope of victory and spoil; the mariner goes to sea, in hope of gain; and so the rest. If you think this hope has no influence into our Christian obedience, hear the Apostle, "He that hath this hope (to be like him) purgeth himself as he is pure," (1 John 3:3). And hear Saint Paul for both the parts of sanctification; "Seeing we have such promises (to be the sons and daughters of God, in the end of the former chapter), let us cleanse ourselves from all filthiness of the flesh and spirit," there's the first; "Perfecting holiness in the fear of God," (2 Corinthians 7:1); then there is the second.

Hope is therefore a special principle of new obedience, and that because, 1. Of the excellence and difficulty of the object, which excite and sharpen diligence, and 2. Also in regard of the delectation and delight, the proper issue of hope, which furthers and quickens operation; as he well observes. They then, that cry down hope, cry down (by consequence) all holiness and obedience. And now, I hope they will consider, they have brought the matter to a fair pass; that by taking away one grace, have subverted all; "Joy, patience, faith, love, and all obedience." But we have more to say yet.

3. The manifest injury they do to a Christian soul, depriving him of so necessary a jewel, as hope is. We will express it by a double metaphor; of a soldier, of a mariner.

1] Of a soldier by land. Our life is a spiritual and continued warfare. There is a panoply, or whole armor commanded to be put on, (Ephesians 6). Among the rest, the "Helmet of Salvation," (Ephesians 6:17), which, what it is, Saint Paul himself tells us in another place, "And for the helmet, the hope of salvation," (1 Thessalonians 5:8). Those then that deny a Christian this use of hope, send him into the field without his helmet, and so expose him to certain danger.

2] Of a mariner, by sea, then hope has a double use under a double metaphor in Scripture:

1) Of the wind, (Hebrews 6:11). The Greek word means *the full gale* (so the word imports) or full assurance of hope. If the Christian soul is a ship (failing in the sea of this world) faith may represent the pilot, and love the sail; but hope is the wind that must fill the sail. Let this pilot be never so confident, the sail spread to the utmost, yet if it desires a good gale of wind, the ship lies becalmed; and her course is ever quicker or slower, as the wind rises or falls. A Christian on earth without hope is a ship at sea without wind.

2) Of an Anchor. "Which hope we have as an Anchor of the soul, sure and steadfast," (Hebrews 6:19). A ship may sometimes have too much, or a contrary wind; and then she has need of an anchor to fix her from being carried away, especially when she draws near to her desired haven. Let faith be the ship, if you will, (and we hear of some that make shipwreck of faith) let love be the merchandise, or passenger, to be conveyed to heaven (when faith and hope, in a sort, cease, and stay behind) yet hope is the anchor, that fixes the ship from being tossed to and fro, and carried away with every wind of doctrine, or wave of

temptation, until love, the passenger or merchandise, has landed in the haven. As the ship with all her tacklings and the anchor lie still at sea, but the passengers and commodities are transported on land. Those then that deny this use of hope, expose the soul to certain danger; either to be calmed for want of wind; or to be carried away, for want of an anchor. If this is enough, hear all:

4. The harshness of the censure, they are like to undergo by this opinion. For if there is no such use of hope, then mark:

1] Either they are not yet converted, but in the state of nature still; as being such as the Apostle says the Ephesians were, "without hope," (Ephesians 2:12) before their conversion.

2] Or else, that they have lost their hope, after once they had it, in conversion; which cannot be, seeing a regenerate man is, "begotten again to a lively hope," (1 Peter 1:3).

3] Or else, (which some do not stick to affirm) that we already have all we hope for; that is, all already glorified. For if we may not hope for any more, it is as if there were no more to be hoped for. And this is it, which some both senselessly and ridiculously have affirmed (and well they may, upon their former opinion) "that our glory in heaven shall be no other, no more, than what we have already, but only in our sense and apprehension." Contrary to the plain text of the Apostle, "We rejoice in hope of the glory of God," (Romans 5:2). These and many more perhaps, are the absurdities wherewith this novel opinion is heavily pressed; which we leave to their more serious consideration. And deliver:

3] The grounds of this their error, as far as we can conceive, and there are these two, the common mothers of most *errors*:

1) Pride, and strange presumption of their own perfection, and of the strength of their own (supposed) love; that they can, and do love God so well, that they need not be beholden to any inferior helps; contrary to the experience of all good hearts, in all times, who were glad and thankful for these supports of the weakness of their imperfect love.

2) Ignorance is the fertile womb of all errors and heresies whatsoever. However these men think themselves wise, and able enough to teach their teachers, yet this opinion manifests a manifold ignorance. We give instance of some of these *particulars:*

(1) Of the true distinction and use of faith, hope, and charity; and that's the reason that faith and love have devoured hope between them. For let me ask them, why do they do good works? They will answer, because they love God. I ask again, why do they love God? Because of their faith by which they believe the goodness of God shown toward them. All this is true, but not enough; for they should have taken in hope in him, because they believe in him. For this is the right order of these graces. The good man is compared to a tree, (Psalm 1) the root of this tree is faith; the stem or body of it, is hope; the branches of it, is love; the fruit of it, are good works. Now it is true indeed, the fruit grows immediately upon the branches, good works proceed from love; but the branches grow next on the stem, and not on the root immediately, that is, love proceeds from hope, and hope from the root of faith. Let them learn this, and then they will not exclude hope but give it its due place.

(2) Of the possible union of a free gift, with a reward. For in this way they seem to reason: *If all is of free gift, then there is no reward; if no reward, then no hope of reward.* But this is their ignorance; free gift and reward agree well enough together; The same thing may be a

free gift, as not being merited by us; and a reward, as so promised by God; and then it is just with him to perform his own promise. The ignorance of this is one cause of the popish merit. Where there is a reward, there is merit, our rhemists say. and these men for fear of merit have utterly renounced all reward; whereas, we say, there is a reward, where there is no merit; and where there is a free gift, there may be a reward notwithstanding, freely promised, and faithfully performed.

(3) Of the right use of the law, to a regenerate man; and this is the source and springhead of all their erroneous conclusions. For if there is no law, it will follow, then, first, there is no use of promises, if no promises, then no reward; if no reward, then no hope of reward. Again, if there is no law, then there are no good works; (for no work is good without a command) if no good works, then no reward; and so no hope. As on the contrary, if there is no law, then no sin; if no sin, then no punishment; if no punishment, then no fear. So that this first absurdity being granted, all the rest will follow; which I earnestly desire they would seriously consider. And so I leave them, and come to a second use of *Justification* of our practice; I mean of us ministers,

who urge upon men, even the best men, the duties of religion, as with fear of punishments on the one side, so with hope of reward on the other side. For which our method, we are by these novelists, styled legal preachers. But I would gladly be resolved by any reasonable man, why we may not as well use the like arguments, as (I say not the Prophets of old) Christ and his Apostles in the New Testament? why may it not be as lawful for me, to exhort men to the patient suffering of persecution, and that with joy, as for our Savior, with the same argument; "For great is your reward in heaven?" Why may I not provoke men to an endeavor of perfect holiness, with remembrance of the promise of God, the object of hope, as Saint Paul did his Corinthians, "Seeing we have these promises," (2 Corinthians 7:1).

3] Admiration, for we are to admire at the never enough admired goodness of God, and contemplate our own badness. His goodness, that will omit no means to do us good; Commands, promises, threatening; to work upon our love, by the goodness of his commands; to persuade our hope by the sweetness of his promises; and (if these will not prevail) to scare us from our wicked courses, by the terrors of his threatening. He might (as Kings) command and expect our obedience; or punish our disobedience; but no means shall be omitted to work us unto good. Our own badness, that will admit scarce any of his means to do ourselves good. Nor commands, nor promises, nor threats can prevail with many (too many of us) either to forsake evil, or do good. What mettle are we made of, that no course can work with us! A King, a mortal man, commands, and we obey; he threatens and we quake; he promises and we run. O! the lamentable badness of our hearts; O the admired goodness of our God!

4] Exhortation; that seeing we know our liberty, we learn to use it; to provoke ourselves to good works, by the hope of the promised reward. Do not be so ignorant, as not to know it; or so proud and presumptuous, as to refuse such gracious helps, as God in mercy has afforded us. We say to you, in the words of Saint Paul, and why may we not? "Cast not away your confidence (which is nothing but a confirmed hope) which hath great recompense of reward," (Hebrews 10:35). And again, "Be not weary of well-doing, for in due season you shall reap, if you faint not," (Galatians 6:9). And with Saint Peter, "Gird up the loins of your mind, and hope to the end." Yet take some cautions with you, for your better directions in the use of your hope. For there is a hope of reward lawful, there is another unlawful; both good and bad are carried with hope of reward, but you shall observe a palpable difference, in these particulars:

(1) A wicked man looks at the present, not regarding the future; at a temporal, not an eternal reward; like that prodigal child, "Father give me the portion of goods," "What profit, (present profit) is there in serving of God," they say, (Malachi 3:14). "Who will shew us any good?" What good? "Corn, and wine, and oil," (Psalm 4), profit, pleasure, honor; not staying or trusting to anything hereafter. But the truly godly man looks at things to come; and like a good child waits till the time appointed of his father; So Saint Paul intimates the difference, "While we look not at the things that are seen (as worldly men do) but at the things which are not seen; For the things which are seen are temporal, but the things which are not seen are eternal," (2 Corinthians 4:18).

(2) Wicked men look at the reward, as a due debt, merited by their formal obedience; "Give me the portion of goods that belongs to me," he said; and therefore, bargain with God for it. The godly expect it,

as a special favor of promise; in all humility acknowledging themselves less than the least of all God's mercies; that's another.

(3) Where there are three things in Scripture to be eyed and observed, the command, the promise, and the threatening; and it is not possible to look on them all at once with two eyes. A wicked man bestows both of his eyes, one upon the threatening, the other upon the promise, but neither upon the command. A godly man, whatever he does with one eye, to bestow it either on the promises or threatening; the other is ever fixed upon the command which difference is apparently by this; that where the command comes without an express promise or threatening, a wicked man will do just nothing, neither forsake evil, nor do good; take a vainglorious man, tell him, God commands him to give alms; if you do not show him with it, you shall have applause and credit from men, if you do it, or a curse attending you, if you do not do it; he lies like a ship at sea, becalmed for lack of wind; or a mill, that moves no longer than the water runs. Yes, that many times, neither promises nor threats can make him stir to perform an express command; which argues that those commands he performs, he does it not out of respect of

the command; but either out of hope of reward or fear of punishment. On the other side, take a good man, tell him, "Thus saith the Lord," this is God's will and command. Though you say nothing of the promise or threatening; he is like the centurion's servant, if he says, "Go," he goes. That's the difference that David intimates, when he says to God; "I have an eye, or respect, to all thy commandments." As a good servant that respects his Master; let strangers say, "Go," or "Come," he does not stir, because he doesn't respect them, though perhaps they promise or threaten; but if his Master but winks with his eye, or nods with his head, intimating his pleasure, he presently runs. The command of God is the wind that fills his sails; as that phrase is elegantly used by the Apostle, "led with all the will of God," (Philippians 4:12); as a sail with wind.

(4) Because wicked men will pretend to follow a conscience of a command. There is yet another difference observable, and that is that where these two meet (as sometimes they do) a command, and a promise; a wicked man does it principally out of the hope of reward, and subordinates the command to his own profit. Take but an instance or two. Balaam goes to Balak, as he was commanded, or rather permitted by

God, but the loadstone that begun this motion was that, "wages of iniquity," (2 Peter 2:15) the reward promised by Balak. The same may be noted in John, who drove furiously in the execution of God's command (as he would seem) on Ahab's family; and in pretense cries, "Come see the zeal." But the first mover of all this fury (rather than zeal) was that message of the Prophet, "Thus saith the Lord, I have anointed thee King over Israel," (2 Kings 9:6-7). The kingdom was principally in his eye; and if he might have safely enjoyed that, without any further danger, I doubt whether Jehoram, and Jezebel, and the rest had died. With a godly man it is quite the contrary; where he has an eye upon the reward, he subordinates that to the command, and uses it only as a help to further his execution of the command. This will the better appear, if we sever the duty from the reward; which meeting together, make it doubtful (to others at least) which most prevails to the motion. For instance, when religion, and prosperity, and peace, and credit meet together, who is almost not religious? And it is a hard matter, for a bystander to say which draws most. Sever them and you shall see straight. Two gentlemen walk together with one man at their heels; what strangers can we say, whom he follows? Follow them until they part, and you shall discover the man to whom he retains. So it is here, if to be religious (in such times, and places, or company) may purchase a wicked man dangers, or disgrace, or scorn, you shall see a hollow heart forsake and almost abjure religion, and swim along with the stream. As the stony ground hearers (Matthew 13) made fair show until persecution arose, and then they were offended; which concludes strongly that they followed religion, but for peace's sake, and not peace for religion. Now a truly good heart is principally drawn by God's command, and entire love to religion; which appears by this, that sever peace and religion, he still keeps on his course; and though the world frowns or scorns, he will follow his religion still. What use then of the hope of reward? Why, indeed, if he may have peace with religion, he likes it well, and is so much more zealous in his profession of it; but if not, he does not care for it, but will rather part with peace than with religion. The hope of reward is in his eye, but by the way, he does not take up his religion for peace, but makes his advantage of peace, to advance his religion. It is a pretty phrase of the Apostle concerning Moses, not, "he cast an eye (after he had made his choice, and was going on his way) upon the recompense of reward," (Hebrews 11:26). Not as a ground of undertaking, but as an *encouragement* of his undertaken journey. As if a father should bid his loving and willing child to go on such an errand; and when he was readily running, should call him back and say; Child, because I see you are so willing to execute my command, here's money to put in your purse, to spend by the way, and here's a horse to carry you with more ease; and hereafter I will promise you, you shall be my heir. This no doubt, must necessarily put joy and spirits into the child, with more cheerfulness to perform his duty; though he had no eye on these in his first setting out. In a word, there are two things that further the motion of a clock, the plummet, and the oil bestowed upon the wheels; the first and chiefest is the plummet, that begins the motion; the next is the oil, and that facilitates the motion. So, be it a good man has an eye to the reward, yet the command of God is the plummet, or prime mover; if he meets with a promise by the way, he uses it as oil to make his motion quicker. The command of God is the principal mover; the hope of reward is but the subordinate helper of his course. And this, I take it, is lawful, against all cavils and exceptions; A man, first looking at God, may in the next place look at himself, and help himself, in the service of God, with the hope of a promised reward.

And this is the thing, I have here intended to urge on you; *the work of religion is not more laborious than the reward promised is glorious.* Do not look so much at the work as at the issue. What, though you see no present profit, verily there is a reward for the righteous. He that sows shall in due season reap. Good works are a seed, which many times seem lost; and we think all is gone. No, they are a seed, which must lie a time underground, before it can come forth. "He that goeth forth and carries good seed, shall come again with joy, and bring his sheaves with him," (Psalm 126:6). I use but this persuasion; the want of this eyeing of the promises of God, is the cause of all, or much of our discontent in our callings, of magistrate, minister, master, servant, etc. when we do not find our labor successful, or that respect which we expected upon our conscionable endeavors. "No man so crossed as I; no man takes so much pains to so little purpose; no man finds such poor respects." Is it not because you look at men, and do not have an eye upon God, and upon the promised recompense of reward? It was a strong weakness and a strange pusillanimity for such a Prophet as Jeremiah, to say upon the non-proficiency of his people, "I will speak no more In the name of the Lord; O! that I had a cottage in a garden of cucumbers." That was heroic of another, his fellow, "I have labored in vain, I have spent my strength in vain; yet surely my judgment is with the Lord, and my work (or reward) with my God," (Isaiah 49:4). My brethren (the Lord's ministers), "...be instant, preach the word, in season, out of season," (1 Peter 5:2-3); do not be discouraged by the unprofitableness or unthankfulness of your people; for you serve a good Master, that will pay you your wages; and the less from them, the more you may expect from him. It is that wherewith the Apostle encourages servants (of unthankful and unnatural masters) to all sincere and faithful obedience, "Servants, obey your masters. And whatsoever ye do, do it heartily, as to the Lord, and not unto men. Knowing that of the Lord, ye shall receive the reward of inheritance; for ye serve the Lord Christ," (Colossians 3:22). The same I say to all estates and conditions of men. Whatsoever you do, do it heartily, knowing that of the Lord you shall receive the reward of inheritance. O!, could we but look up at God, and his promise of reward, by the eye of our hope, how easily might we in our callings pass through good report and ill report, good respect and disrespect, and trample all the unthankfulness of men under our feet! I conclude all with the words of the Apostle, "Wherefore, my dear brethren, be ye constant, unmoveable, always abounding in the work of the Lord, forasmuch as ye know that your labor shall not be in vain in the Lord," (1 Corinthians 15:58).

www.ingramcontent.com/pod-product-compliance
Lightning Source LLC
Chambersburg PA
CBHW030047100426
42734CB00036B/386